Forget-Me-Not Bible Story Activities

by Christine Yount

Group

Loveland, Colorado

To all those uniquely created children
who'll find great joy in discovering God's truths in
the way they learn best!

· ·

Forget-Me-Not Bible Story Activities
Copyright © 1997 Christine Yount

Credits
Editor: Jennifer Root Wilger
Senior Editor: Paul Woods
Chief Creative Officer: Joani Schultz
Copy Editor: Julie Meiklejohn
Art Director: Lisa Chandler
Cover Art Director: Helen H. Lannis
Cover Designer: Diana Walters
Computer Graphic Artist: Joyce Douglas
Illustrator: Rex Bohn
Production Manager: Ann Marie Gordon

Unless otherwise noted, Scriptures quoted from The Youth Bible, New Century Version,
copyright © 1991 by Word Publishing, Dallas, Texas, 75039. Used by permission.

Library of Congress Cataloging-in-Publication Data
Yount, Christine.
        Forget-me-not Bible story activities / by Christine Yount.
                p.   cm.
        ISBN 1-55945-633-7
        1. Bible games and puzzles. 2. Bible--Study and teaching.
    3. Christian education of children. 4. Creative activities and seat
    work.   I. Title.
    GV1507.B5Y68   1997
    220'.071--dc21   97-8984
                                                                              CIP

10 9 8 7 6 5 4 3 2   06 05 04 03 02 01 00 99 98 97
Printed in the United States of America.

ontents

Introduction 4

In the Beginning, God Created (Genesis 1:1–2:3) 8

The First Family (Genesis 2:4–3:24) 12

A Floating Zoo (Genesis 6:1–9:17) 16

If You Build It, Will God Come? (Genesis 11:1-9) 21

Sold Into Slavery (Genesis 37:1–45:28) 26

Free at Last (Exodus 3:1–12:51) 30

Let Freedom Ring (Exodus 12:31–15:21) .36

Tumbling Down (Joshua 6:2-20) 42

Sapped Strength (Judges 16:4-30) 46

A Woman of Excellence (Ruth 1:1–4:22) 51

Giant Removal (1 Samuel 17:1-58) 55

Heroine of the Day (Esther 2:1–8:17) 58

What's for Lunch? (Daniel 6:1-28) 63

Swallowed Up (Jonah 1:1–3:10) 69

Preparing the Way (Matthew 3:1-15) 73

Anything's Possible (Mark 6:45-56) 77

A Savior Is Born (Luke 2:1-20) 80

Clean Again (Luke 17:11-19) 84

All Hope is Gone (Luke 23:1-56) 88

Alive Again! (Luke 24:1-49) 92

Hold Everything! (John 11:1-44) 95

I Saw the Light (Acts 9:1-22) 98

Jailhouse Rock (Acts 16:16-34) 102

Shipwrecked (Acts 27:27–28:5) 106

Introduction

You're reading the lesson plan for this week's lesson. Under your breath, you pray, "Please God, not another collage!"

"Who writes these lessons, anyway? They sure don't know my kids—and how antsy they get when they can't move around. And my kids hate music. I lose half the class every time we have to spend so much time singing. But that's better than trying to lead a class discussion—getting responses is like pulling teeth. I'm sure I could do a better job of writing lessons for my kids. But who has the time?"

If you've ever felt this way, stop settling for less than the best. Here's a new resource to help you customize your curriculum to better fit your class's needs. Simply open *Forget-Me-Not Bible Story Activities* to the Bible story you're covering this week. Then choose the activities that fit the ways the kids in your class learn best. You may even decide to throw your original lesson out the window and combine all seven Forget-Me-Not activities to create a complete lesson. After all, who knows your kids and what they need better than you do?

As the editor of Children's Ministry Magazine, I've found that most teachers revamp existing lesson plans, rather than teach them "as is." *Forget-Me-Not Bible Story Activities* will provide you with complete lesson plans, or you can use individual activities to supplement and enhance your existing curriculum. Each Forget-Me-Not lesson includes seven brand-new ideas and an "Extra! Extra!" box that you can use to give kids even more. And at least one activity in each lesson includes a fresh, new way to tell the Bible story. No more flannel graphs, filmstrips, or monotone reading.

Kids won't forget the activities in this book. That's because each activity focuses on a different learning style. No child will be excluded from a lesson because it doesn't fit the way he or she learns. Does your class "chat up a storm?" Then try a verbal or interpersonal activity. Group got the wiggles? Pull out a physical activity. Chairs full of strong, silent types? Let them relax with reflective activities designed just for them. Not sure where your kids fit in? Then check out the "How Kids Learn" section on page 6.

Verbal, visual, interpersonal, physical, musical, reflective, and logical learners will be delighted by the activities in this book. Each activity is marked with a corresponding learning-style symbol so you can quickly find just the right one. And if you use all seven activities together, your entire class will be gripped by God's Word in the ways they learn best!

Your kids will love mixing up a colored-gelatin rainbow, calculating how the Tower of Babel may have been built, or making a music video about Jesus' resurrection. They'll squirm as they spread "leprosy" on each other's skin, giggle as they create locust concoctions, and smile as they affirm each other's Christlike qualities. Guaranteed: You'll find fun, creative ideas to get your kids excited about learning God's Word—even those kids who've been in church since birth.

So thumb through the pages of this book. Choose the activities that will work for your class. Your kids will never forget 'em. And neither will you!

How Kids Learn

To get a feel for the ways the children in your classroom learn best, review the learning-style characteristics listed below. Then complete the "How *Your* Kids Learn" chart on page 7 to determine which activities would be best to use with the kids in your class this week.

 **Verbal**

This child:
tells stories
has a good memory
enjoys word games
enjoys reading and writing
has a good vocabulary
communicates well

Logical

This child:
wants to know how things work
is good at "mental math"
enjoys math activities
enjoys strategy games
enjoys brain teasers

 **Visual**

This child:
reads maps, charts, and
    diagrams easily
enjoys art activities
likes visual presentations
enjoys puzzles and mazes
doodles on paper

Musical

This child:
remembers melodies
recognizes off-key music
plays a musical instrument or
    sings in a choir
speaks or moves rhythmically
responds favorably to music
sings a lot

 **Physical**

This child:
excels in sports
moves or fidgets when seated
enjoys hands-on activities
enjoys physical activity
expresses him- or herself
    dramatically
enjoys working with clay and
    finger painting

 Interpersonal

This child:
enjoys being with friends
acts as a natural leader
belongs to many clubs
likes to play games with others
shows concern for others

Reflective

This child:
is independent
has a good sense of his or her
    own personal strengths and
    weaknesses
prefers working alone
has high self-esteem
is interested in knowing him- or
    herself better

ow *Your* Kids Learn

Think about each child in your classroom, and list each child's name on the chart below. Then mark the learning styles in which each child displays one or more of the characteristics on the previous page.

When you've finished, review the learning styles you've marked, and tailor your lessons to reach students with those learning styles. Most kids will probably display characteristics in several different learning styles. But usually each child is "smartest" in one or two learning styles. And kids enjoy learning best when they can use their "smarts."

Name	Verbal	Logical	Visual	Physical	Musical	Interpersonal	Reflective

In the Beginning, God Created

Kids will explore their God-given creativity as they discover the variety of wonderful things God created for them to enjoy.

Musical

Supplies: Bibles, a cassette recorder, and a blank cassette tape

Preparation: none

Tell kids that they're going to help re-create the sounds of Creation using items found in your room.

Form three groups. Label the groups A, B, and C. Distribute Bibles to kids, and assign groups the following Scriptures:

Group A—Genesis 1:1-5 (Day 1) and Genesis 1:6-8 (Day 2)
Group B—Genesis 1:9-13 (Day 3) and Genesis 1:14-19 (Day 4)
Group C—Genesis 1:20-23 (Day 5) and Genesis 1:24-31 (Day 6)

Have kids in each group read their assigned Scriptures and brainstorm sounds that might have been heard during those portions of Creation. Help groups find materials to create their sounds.

After five minutes, have groups take turns recording their creation sounds on a blank cassette tape with a cassette recorder, beginning with sounds from Day 1. When each group has recorded its sounds, bring the groups together for a lively reading of the Creation story. Read each Scripture passage, pausing as needed to play the recorded sounds.

After you finish the entire passage, ask:

● **What do you think it would have been like to be there as God created the world?**

● **What other sounds do you think you might've heard?**

● **Why do you think God created so many different sounds in the world?**

Say: **You all did a great job with your creation sounds. Let's use the sound of clapping to thank God for creating so many different sounds for us to enjoy.**

Lead kids in clapping.

Visual

Supplies: Plates; plastic knives; napkins; sugar ice-cream cones; bowls of green frosting; and small candies such as M&M's, gumdrops, Skittles, and Life Savers

Preparation: none

Set out the bowls of green frosting, plastic knives, and small candies. Give each child a plate and a sugar cone. Have children turn their cones upside-down on their plates. Then have them spread the green frosting over the cones to create "trees." Children may use the candies to add fruit or flowers to their trees.

As children work, talk about all the different kinds of trees God created. Point out that trees grow brand-new leaves each year.

When children have finished decorating their trees, say: **Just as every person's** tree is different, every tree God made is different. Some have leaves, others have needles and pine cones. Some produce flowers, and some produce berries or fruit that are good to eat. These trees you've made look very tasty. Let's enjoy some of their fruit now.

Invite a volunteer to offer a prayer of thanks and then have kids enjoy eating the trees! Hand out napkins for kids to clean their hands with after they're finished.

VeRBaL

Supplies: none

Preparation: none

Form groups of four. Have groups discuss what it might have been like to live in the Garden of Eden. Encourage them to consider the following elements:
- Where would you sleep?
- What would you eat?
- What games would you play?
- How would you interact with the animals?

After a few minutes, regain kids' attention, and say: **The Bible doesn't tell us very much about the garden God created. But it does tell us that God created the people who lived in the garden in his own image. That means people can think and be creative too. Right now, I'd like you to have fun with your own creative imaginations. Work with the others in your group to make up a story about a day in the Garden of Eden. In a few minutes, we'll share our stories with each other.**

Have groups take turns telling their stories and then thank God for the gift of creativity.

LogiCaL

Supplies: Bibles, pencils, paper, and a chalkboard and chalk or newsprint and a marker

Preparation: Write the following questions on a chalkboard or a sheet of newsprint.

- According to the Bible, how did the earth and all that's in it get here?
- What does this psalm say that God made?
- What does this psalm say that God is doing now?

Invite two science teachers, scientists, or other adults to debate the theories of Creation and evolution. Instruct your volunteers to keep their debate simple and straightforward and to limit it to no more than ten minutes.

Introduce the topic and the debaters to your class. Let your guests debate for ten minutes and then call time. Allow a few minutes for kids to ask questions and then lead them in thanking your debaters.

Form groups of four, and give each group pencils, paper, and Bibles. Have each group choose a Reader (reads the Scripture out loud for the group), a Scribe (writes group answers), a Question Asker (asks the questions for the group to answer), and a Timekeeper (makes sure the task is completed on time).

Have Readers read Psalm 104 for their groups. Then have Question Askers ask the questions listed on the newsprint or chalkboard for their groups to answer.

Instruct Timekeepers to watch the clock and allow the group to spend no more than four minutes answering each question. Allow no more than twelve minutes total for groups to complete their studies. Then review the questions with the whole class. Encourage Scribes to report their groups' answers.

After you've discussed all the questions, say: **According to this psalm, God made everything in our world. From the gentle sparrow to the roaring lion, God knew exactly what each creation would need to live a healthy and happy life. God knows exactly what we need, too, and we can trust him to take care of us.**

✋ PHYSICAL

Supplies: A whistle

Preparation: none

Play Creation Tag. Choose one child to be "It," and have that child try to tag each player. (If you're playing inside, you may want to have kids shuffle or hop instead of running.) As kids play, call out creation categories, one at a time, from the list below. Each child can avoid being tagged by kneeling on one knee and naming an item in the category you mentioned. For example, if the creation category is farm animals, the child may kneel on one knee and say "cow." No item can be repeated. When a child is tagged, he or she will freeze in a pose which represents something in the named creation category until a new category is named. For example, if the creation category is trees, a tagged child could pose like a tree with his or her arms out over his or her head like branches.

Use the following creation categories, or make up additional categories of your own.

- trees
- vegetables
- insects
- jungle animals
- sea animals
- fruits
- bodies of water
- birds
- farm animals

Blow a whistle to change creation categories every minute or two. After you've played the game several times, wrap up the activity by saying: **Wow! Even though we named a lot of different creations, we only mentioned a small fraction of the bugs, birds, animals, and plants God created. Our planet is full of life and activity, just as our room was full of activity as we played our game.**

If this is your last activity, have kids strike their favorite insect or animal poses as you pray and thank God for the variety of life he created.

👥 INTERPERSONAL

Supplies: A Bible, paper, markers or crayons, and tape or pins

Preparation: none

Form pairs. Have each pair work together to create and name a new animal. Encourage kids to imagine what sound their animals would make, what they would eat, where they would live, and what they would look like. Distribute paper and markers or crayons, and have pairs draw pictures of their animals.

After pairs have created and named their animals, have pairs combine to form groups of four. Have each pair in a group introduce its animal to the other pair.

Then have groups discuss the following questions, one at a time:
- **How easy or difficult was it to create a new animal?**
- **How do you think your process of creating an animal was like the way God created animals? How was it different?**
- **What does your creation say about you?**
- **What does God's creation say about God?**

Regain kids' attention, and invite them to report on their discussions to the whole group. Then have kids return to their original pairs. Read aloud Romans 1:20. Say: **The beautiful things that God has made reveal things to us about who God is. Tell your partner about a time you've been in a beautiful place in nature. Did you feel close to God at that time? Why or why not?**

Allow time for partners to share and then continue by saying: **Share with your partner your answer to each of these questions:**
- **Nature has harmony and order. What does that reveal to us about our Creator?**
- **Think about how quiet it can be in nature. What does that tell us about God?**

After pairs have finished their discussions, close by saying: **Be alert this week and look at and listen to God's creation so you can learn more about what God is like.** Tape or pin kids' animal pictures up in your classroom.

Reflective

Supplies: Paper, pencils, newsprint, a marker, and tape or pins

Preparation: Prepare a newsprint chart that lists what was created on each day of Creation. Post the chart where kids can refer to it as they complete this activity.

Set out paper and pencils. Have kids copy and complete this statement: "My favorite day of creation would be _____ because _____."

Circulate among kids to offer help as needed. Allow at least five minutes of quiet time for kids to complete this activity. After kids have finished, invite them to share their responses if they want to. Or invite kids to post their finished statements on a "Favorite Days" wall or bulletin board.

Close by thanking God for the unique creations of each day of Creation and for each unique child in your class.

EXTRA! EXTRA! EXTRA! EXTRA! EXTRA!

- Serve herbal sun-tea and fresh fruit. Explain to children that God's sun warmed the water to make the tea.

- Sing "Hip Hip Hooray," a song about creation, written and recorded by Mary Rice Hopkins.

- Teach this lesson outside in a beautifully landscaped area such as a park or garden.

EXTRA! EXTRA! EXTRA! EXTRA! EXTRA!

The First Family

Kids will discover the harmful consequences of sin and temptation as they explore the events that took place in the Garden of Eden.

PHYSICAL

Supplies: A Bible; a dollar bill for each child; and a beautifully wrapped "dud" gift, such as a pile of rocks, a shovelful of dirt, or a stack of old newspapers

Preparation: If you'll be playing in a classroom, clear the room of furniture and other objects kids could trip over. If possible, arrange to play the game in a gymnasium or outside.

Read aloud Genesis 2:7-8, 20-22. Say: **God created Adam and Eve, and God gave them the choice to obey him or to disobey him. Listen to how Adam and Eve chose to disobey.**

Read aloud Genesis 3:1-6. Hold up the wrapped gift, and say: **Just as Adam and Eve had choices, we have choices today. We're going to play a game of choices. As a part of our game, you'll each get a dollar bill. You can choose to keep your dollar, or you can choose to try to get this gift. If you choose to keep your dollar, you'll be safe. If you choose to try to get the gift, you'll risk losing your dollar. If you're caught while you're trying to get the gift, you'll have to give me your dollar.**

Give each child a dollar bill. (If you have a large class, you may want to use quarters instead of dollar bills.) Choose one child to be "It." Have It stand at one end of the room and face the wall. Have the other children stand against the opposite wall and face It. Place the wrapped gift about three feet behind It.

Give a signal and allow children to move toward the gift if they want to risk losing their dollar bills. If It turns around and sees kids moving, they have been caught and they have to return their dollars to you. As long as It doesn't catch them moving, they can continue on. The game is over when one person reaches the gift or everyone has been caught.

After the game, collect the dollar bills from kids who didn't lose them during the game. Then unwrap the gift, and read aloud Genesis 3:6. Ask:

● **Eve was tempted by the beautiful fruit on the tree. How tempted were you to try to get the beautifully wrapped box? Explain.**

Read aloud Genesis 3:8-19, 23-24. Ask:

● **When Adam and Eve were caught in their sin, they were afraid. When you were caught during our game, how did you feel?**

● **How did you feel when you discovered what was in the box?**

● **How is that like Adam and Eve may have felt when they discovered the result of disobeying God and eating the fruit?**

● **Eating the fruit was a big temptation for Adam and Eve. What temptations do kids your age have?**

● **When Adam and Eve gave in to temptation, they were forced to leave the Garden of Eden. What happens to you when you give in to temptation?**

Close the activity by praying about specific temptations kids have mentioned. Ask God to give kids grace and strength to obey him every day.

VISUAL AND VERBAL

Supplies: Sample travel brochures or magazine advertisements for vacation spots, magazines, scissors, paper, markers or crayons, and tape or pins

Preparation: none

Form groups of four. Show the kids the sample travel brochures or magazine advertisements, and distribute paper, magazines, scissors, and markers or crayons. Have each group create its own travel brochure for the Garden of Eden, complete with graphics, pictures, and text. Encourage groups to create brochures for Eden that would entice people to go there. For example, groups may brag about the beautiful gardens or the luscious fruit.

When groups finish, have them present their brochures to the rest of the class.

After the presentations, say: **Eden was a beautiful place. As you've seen by these exciting travel brochures, it had beautiful gardens and tasty fruit to eat. It probably had more animals than any zoo or safari park in our world today. But because of Adam and Eve's disobedience, no one will ever get to vacation there.**

Have kids use red crayons or markers to mark their brochures "Attraction Closed," "Closed to the Public," or "Shut Down by Sin." Post the brochures on a wall or bulletin board to remind kids of the consequences of disobedience.

MUSICAL

Supplies: Bibles; cassettes or CDs in a variety of musical styles such as classical, country, contemporary, Christian, rock, or folk; and two cassette or CD players

Preparation: Before class, listen to and select a wide variety of musical selections to ensure kids will have appropriate music to choose from.

Form two groups. Make sure each group has at least one Bible and one cassette or CD player. Put the CDs and tapes in an area that is easily accessible to both groups. Assign Genesis 2 to one group and Genesis 3 to the other group.

Tell members of each group that they'll be working together to create a musical score for their Bible passage. Explain that a musical score is the music we hear in the background of a movie. Point out that when the story is exciting, the music is fast. When the story is sad, the music is slow. Invite kids to describe or hum any movie music they remember. You might want to show kids a few video snippets to demonstrate the importance of a movie's musical score. If you choose to do this, be sure to obtain permission from the videos' distribution companies prior to using the videos.

Have groups read their chapters and identify happy, sad, exciting, or scary events. You may need to help kids do this. Then have groups listen to music and choose an appropriate musical selection for each event. If you're using cassette tapes, have kids cue the tapes to the selections they've chosen.

When groups are ready, read the Bible passages aloud. As you read, have groups play their musical selections at the appropriate times.

Logical

Supplies: Bibles, paper, and pencils

Preparation: Invite your pastor or another teacher to join you for this activity.

Form three groups. Label the groups Bananas, Apples, and Pears. Then have kids make "fruit salads" by forming trios including one child from each of the three groups. It's okay to have more than one of each "fruit" in a trio.

Give each trio a Bible, paper, and pencils, and have each trio brainstorm three "stumper" questions to ask God about the Bible story. For example, kids may ask, "Why did you allow temptation?" or "Why did you create Adam and Eve if you knew they were going to choose to sin?"

Allow up to ten minutes for trios to create their stumper questions. Then call kids back together, and introduce the pastor or teacher you've invited to join you. Let kids take turns asking their questions, and do your best to answer them along with the pastor or teacher. Encourage kids to contribute to the discussion if they have ideas about each other's questions. If you encounter a question you don't feel you can answer, feel free to use "R & R"— *Research* the question and *Return* with an answer the next time you meet.

After you've gone through all the questions, say: **Wow! Those were tough questions. I wonder if Adam and Eve asked God any of those questions when they were tempted in the garden. It's great that God gave us minds to think, ask questions, and make choices. If you're tempted this week, think first, ask yourself questions about what will happen if you give in to the temptation, and then choose your actions wisely!**

Interpersonal

Supplies: none

Preparation: none

Form pairs. Say: **All of us have been tempted to disobey God—just as Adam and Eve were tempted in the garden. Adam and Eve faced serious consequences because of their choice to sin.**

Ask:

● **What were the consequences of Adam and Eve's disobedience?**

Say: **Turn to your partner, and tell him or her about a time you disobeyed God. What were the consequences of your disobedience?**

Allow a few minutes for pairs to share. Then regain kids' attention, and say: **Now tell your partner what you could have done differently in your situation. What will you do the next time you're tempted to disobey?**

Allow a few minutes for pairs to share. Encourage kids to pray for their partners if they want to.

REFLECTIVE

Supplies: A Bible

Preparation: none

Read 1 John 1:9. Say: **Adam and Eve aren't the only ones who've sinned. The Bible says that everyone on earth has sinned and fallen short of God's perfection. But in this verse, God tells us that he will forgive us if we confess our sins to him. To confess means to agree with God. When we confess our sins, we're agreeing with God that the wrong things we've done, said, or thought are sin in his eyes. Let's take about two minutes to pray to God silently and confess any sin that we've committed.**

Allow two minutes for silent prayer. Then bring kids together and thank God for his cleansing forgiveness that helps each person start anew.

EXTRA! EXTRA! EXTRA! EXTRA! EXTRA!

● Create a fun play with overhead transparencies by using the "Adam and Eve" skit in *Big Action Bible Skits* (available from Group Publishing).

● Play Don Francisco's song "Adam, Where Are You?" Afterward, have kids discuss their feelings as they listened to the song and how they would've felt if they had been Adam.

● Read Christina Rossetti's poem *Goblin Market*. Lead children in comparing and contrasting the poem with the account of the Fall.

● Provide things that would grow in a garden as snacks, such as sliced veggies, sliced fruit, or granola.

EXTRA! EXTRA! EXTRA! EXTRA! EXTRA!

 **A** **Floating Zoo**

Kids will learn
about God's
faithfulness as
they discover
how God took
care of Noah
during the flood.

EXTRA! EXTRA! EXTRA! EXTRA! EXTRA!

● Let kids sit back and enjoy the show! Invite three adults to prepare and then present the following short skit for your class. Encourage your actors to dress for their parts.

● You'll need to be prepared to spray the spray bottle and flash the lights at the end of the skit. For added effect, provide extra spray bottles and invite additional volunteers to help with the spraying.

EXTRA! EXTRA! EXTRA! EXTRA! EXTRA!

Famous Last Words

Props: You'll need two chairs, a piece of lumber, a hammer, and a spray bottle filled with water.

Characters:

Noah, an old man
Ehu and Yahu, Noah's neighbors (male or female, any age)

Script

(Ehu and Yahu are sitting in chairs.)

Yahu: Have you heard the latest joke?

Ehu: No, what is it?

Yahu: What's brown all over and full of nuts?

Ehu: I don't know. What?

Yahu: Noah's big boat!

(Both laugh.)

(Noah walks across the stage carrying a piece of lumber and a hammer.)

Noah: Good morning, neighbors.

(Ehu and Yahu snicker.)

Ehu and Yahu: *(Sarcastically)* Good morning, Noah.

Noah: I'm on my way to put the finishing touches on the ark.

Ehu: We were just talking about that.

Noah: Oh, really? I hope you were saying that you'll join my family and me before the rains come.

Yahu: *(Sarcastically)* Oh yeah, all right! That's exactly what we were saying.

(Both laugh.)

Noah: God has promised, and he is faithful. It won't be long before the rains come. *(Looks up)* Then, my friends, it will be too late. Come with me now.

Ehu: Noah, we're not going to get any rain. You're losing it, man! Why don't you just knock it off?

Noah: *(Distracted)* I must go. I have animals to corral.

Yahu: Yeah, yeah, yeah. Go get on with your monkey business...

(Noah walks out of the room.)

(Water sprays over Ehu, Yahu, and the class.)

Yahu: Hey, what was that?

(Both look scared.)

(Flash the lights several times. Then turn them off for twenty seconds before turning them back on.)

THE END

After the skit, paraphrase the story of Noah's ark from Genesis 6:1–9:17. Tell children they'll be participating in many fun activities to learn more about this story.

👁 Visual

Supplies: A Bible; clear plastic cups; blunt plastic knives; plastic spoons; six rectangular pans; and fruit-flavored gelatin in the following flavors: lemon, strawberry, lime, blueberry, grape, and orange

Preparation: Before class, prepare the gelatin according to the package instructions. Fill the pans no more than one-half inch full of gelatin.

Have kids use blunt plastic knives to cut the gelatin into small squares. Then have kids layer the gelatin squares in clear plastic cups. As kids work, have them imagine they're creating rainbows.

When all the gelatin has been layered in the cups, give kids plastic spoons and have them enjoy their rainbow snacks. As kids eat, say: **After Noah's ark landed, God had a very special message for Noah. Listen as I read it.**

Read aloud Genesis 9:8-17. Say: **Every time you see a rainbow, remember God's faithfulness to Noah. Thank God that he loves us and will never again destroy the earth with a flood.**

🎵 Musical

Supplies: Rhythm instruments (optional)

Preparation: Practice singing the song below so that you can teach it to your class.

Form three groups. Teach children this song to the tune of "Row, Row, Row Your Boat." If you'd like, write out the words on newsprint or a chalkboard. Have each group make up motions to go with the song. Kids will also enjoy using rhythm instruments if you have them available. Once groups have created their motions, bring kids back together and have each group sing the song and display its motions for the rest of the class.

Build, build, build an ark
Out of gopher wood.
God told Noah, "Build an ark;
I'm going to send a flood."

Two, two, two by two;
The animals came in pairs—
Monkeys, elephants, hamsters, sheep,
Lions, tigers, and bears.

The rain, rain, rain came down;
The waters were so high.
It dried up after forty days,
And a rainbow filled the sky.

After each group has presented its motions, have all of the groups sing the song once more and do their motions simultaneously. Then have kids applaud for each other and sit down for a quick rest. Say: **There was a lot of activity going on with all those motions—but probably not as much activity as Noah had with all the animals on the ark. Things must have gotten a little crazy on the ark, but God kept everyone safe until the water dried up. When I count to three, do your favorite motion from our song and shout, "Yeah, God!" Ready? One, two, three!**
Lead kids in cheering for God.

 Verbal

Supplies: Bibles, newsprint and a marker or a chalkboard and chalk, paper, and pencils

Preparation: none

Have kids brainstorm five possible newspaper headlines about the Flood; for example, the headlines might read, "Giant Flood Wipes Out World: Noah Says 'God Did It' " or "Noah Warns the World; Nobody Listens." Write kids' headlines on a sheet of newsprint or a chalkboard.

Form groups of four, and give each group at least one Bible, paper, and pencils. Have each group read the story of the Flood from Genesis 6:1–8:22 and then choose a headline and write a news story about the Flood. Have groups keep their stories to no more than four paragraphs. Then have each group pair up with one other group, and have groups share their news accounts with each other.

After groups have shared, call everyone back together and say: **Although they didn't have newspapers in Noah's day, I'm sure the word got around about the big boat Noah was building. But even though people made fun of him, Noah still followed God's directions. God wants us to follow his directions, too. Choose a partner in your group, and tell him or her one way you'll follow God's directions this week.**

Allow time for kids to share and then ask a volunteer to pray that kids will follow God's directions as Noah did.

Physical

Supplies: A Bible and small plastic building blocks, such as Lego blocks

Preparation: Collect as many small plastic building blocks as you can. You may want to put a note on a church bulletin board, in your church bulletin, or in your church nursery requesting small plastic building blocks.

Have one child read aloud Genesis 6:14-16. Then have kids work together to create a replica of the ark using the small plastic building blocks. If the translation of the Bible you're reading from uses the word "cubit," explain that a cubit equals about eighteen inches. Then step back and let children decide for themselves how to re-create the ark in miniature.

When children have finished, say: **Whew! It took a lot of work to build our ark. Imagine how much time and work it took for Noah to build an ark big enough to hold all the animals! It's a good thing God gave Noah directions!**

After class, you may want to display the finished ark replica in your church foyer or office for families and other church members to see. Be sure to post a note near the replica listing the names of all the children who worked on it.

⚹ LogicaL

Supplies: A small tub of water, towels, a sponge, a plastic lid, a bath toy, a spoon, a pencil, a piece of aluminum foil, a rock, a clear wide-mouthed jar, a salt shaker with salt in it, and a raw egg

Preparation: none

Place the small tub of water on the towels, and set out the sponge, the plastic lid, the bath toy, the spoon, the pencil, the aluminum foil, and the rock. Have kids test the items to determine which ones will float. After each attempt, have children explain why the object did or did not float.

Then set out the clear wide-mouthed jar and the egg. Fill the jar half-full of water. Ask a volunteer to gently set the egg in the water. Ask:
- **Why doesn't the egg float?**
- **How do you think Noah would've felt if his boat hadn't floated?**
- **What would have been necessary to make a boat the size of Noah's float?**

Say: **Let's see what we can do to get our egg to float.**

Use the spoon to lift the egg out of the water and then stir some salt into the water. Set the egg back into the water to see if it will float. Continue this process until the egg floats. Explain to children that the salt makes the water heavier. When an egg-sized volume of water becomes heavier than the egg, the egg will float.

Say: **We're not sure if there was lots of salt in the water that came in Noah's day. But we are sure that there was plenty of water to float Noah's boat. And we know that God's directions helped Noah build a boat that would float—because the ark floated for 150 days.**

When Noah was building the ark, he probably had a lot of questions. He had no idea how much rain would come, how high the water would rise, or whether the ark would carry the weight of all the animals. But he trusted that God could handle all those things. God can handle the questions we have about things in our lives, too.

⊕ ReFLective

Supplies: Paper and crayons or markers

Preparation: none

Set out paper and crayons or markers. Have each child list or draw pictures of the five things he or she would save if a flood threatened his or her home.

Ask kids not to talk during this activity. When kids finish their lists or drawings, encourage them to thank God for giving them their special things and for promising never to flood the whole world again.

INTeRPeRSeNAL

Supplies: A Bible, paper and pencils (if needed), newsprint and a marker or a chalkboard and chalk

Preparation: Copy the following questions onto a sheet of newsprint or a chalkboard.

- Why would you save the items you listed?
- Why are these things important to you?
- Why did God save what he saved?
- Why were these things important to God?

If you didn't do the Reflective activity, distribute paper and pencils and have each child quickly list five things he or she would save if a flood threatened his or her home. Have children share their lists with partners. After pairs have shared their lists, have them discuss the questions listed on the newsprint or chalkboard.

Say: **God wants people to be saved from destruction so they can live with him in heaven.**

Ask:

- **In Noah's day, the ark saved Noah and his family from destruction. How can people be saved from destruction today?**
- **How does Jesus save people from destruction?**

Lead kids in discussing how Jesus' death and resurrection saves us from destruction by providing forgiveness for our sins. If kids are interested, you may want to read additional Scriptures, such as John 3:16; Romans 3:23-26; or Colossians 1:20-22.

Encourage partners to tell each other about people they can tell about Jesus' death and resurrection. Then have partners pray together, thanking God for caring enough to save people from destruction.

EXTRA! EXTRA! EXTRA! EXTRA! EXTRA!

- Create a fun play with overhead transparencies by using the "Noah and the Ark" skit in *Big Action Bible Skits* (available from Group Publishing).

- Build a cardboard ark out of appliance boxes.

- Complete this lesson in a boat in your church parking lot.

- Read *Noah, Noah, What'll We Do?*, a fun foldover book from Group Publishing.

EXTRA! EXTRA! EXTRA! EXTRA! EXTRA!

If You Build It, Will God Come?

As they explore the disastrous effects of the Tower of Babel, kids will learn that God is pleased when his people work together for the right reasons.

Visual

Supplies: A Bible, one copy of the "Brick-Making Instructions" box, potters' clay (available in craft and hobby stores), two cookie sheets, a rolling pin, a ruler, a blunt knife, and an oven

Preparation: Photocopy and cut out the "Brick-Making Instructions" box below, and post it near the kids' work area. Arrange to use your church's oven to bake the bricks. If your church doesn't have an oven, you may want to consider completing this lesson in a church member's home.

Set out the brick-making supplies, and direct kids to their work area. Encourage kids to work together as they follow the instructions. Point out examples of good cooperation as kids work. Allow no more than fifteen minutes for kids to prepare the bricks for baking.

Brick-Making Instructions

On one cookie sheet, roll out the potters' clay to ½ inch thick. Cut the clay into small squares, about ½ inch by ¾ inch. Separate the bricks with a blunt knife. Put the finished bricks on another cookie sheet.

Bake the bricks in an oven on the self-cleaning function for one hour. If your oven doesn't have a self-cleaning function, bake the bricks at the highest possible temperature.

As the bricks are baking, gather kids together and ask them to give reasons they might work together to build a tower using bricks. Kids may give answers such as "to climb it and see farther" or "to create an object of beauty for everyone to enjoy."

After you've heard a few responses, read aloud Genesis 11:1-9. Ask:

● **Why did these people want to build this tower?**

● **Why was God unhappy with their reason for building it?**

● **Do you think God was pleased that the people were working so well together? Why or why not?**

Say: **The people in this story were working together. But they were working together for the wrong reasons. Instead of working together to serve God or to help others, they worked to build a tower that they hoped would increase their own fame. God was not pleased with their attitudes, so he confused their language and separated them.**

Ask:

● **What do you think about what God did to the people? Was it fair? Why or why not?**

● **What reasons for people working together would be pleasing to God?**

Say: **Each time we come to this class, we work together to learn more about God. At home, we work with our families to make our homes pleasant places to live. At school, we work with friends and teachers on assignments to help us learn. God has given us all kinds of neat ways to work together! Be on the lookout for ways you can please God by working with others this week.**

Continue with the rest of your lesson while the bricks finish baking. At the end of class, give a brick to each child. Encourage kids to keep their bricks as a reminder that God wants us to work together for the right reasons.

MUSICAL

Supplies: A CD or cassette player and a CD or cassette tape of "Jesus Loves Me" (optional)

Preparation: Practice speaking and singing the Spanish words to "Jesus Loves Me," following the pronunciation guide below. If you know a person who speaks Spanish, consider inviting him or her to help with this activity!

Teach children to sing the chorus of "Jesus Loves Me" in Spanish.

CRISTO ME AMA
(Jesus Loves Me)

Si, Cristo me ama. *(See KREE-stoh may AH-ma)*
Si, Cristo me ama.
Si, Cristo me ama.
La Biblia dice asi. *(La BEEB-lee-ah DEE-say ah-see)*

Afterward, ask:
● **How did it feel to sing in another language?**
● **How do you think the people at the Tower of Babel felt when they all started speaking in different languages?**
● **What would you have done if all of a sudden you couldn't speak the same language as the people around you?**
Say: **It's very humbling to try to speak a language you don't know. When the pride of the people at Babel caused them to rely on them-selves instead of depending on God, God used language to teach them an important lesson about humility. Now people speak many different languages. Most people can only understand one or a few, but God understands them all!**

Close this activity by singing "Cristo Me Ama," followed by "Jesus Loves Me."

VERBAL

Supplies: Bibles and newsprint and a marker or a chalkboard and chalk

Preparation: none

Form groups of four. Make sure each group has at least one Bible. Have each group make up its own language. For example, groups may choose to use pig Latin, drop first letters of words, or have every word start with the letter H. Give groups ten minutes to develop their languages. Encourage members of each group to practice speaking their language by reading Philippians 2:1-11 out loud in their language.

After about ten minutes, create jigsaw groups with each group including one person from each of the original groups. Have children use their made-up languages as they read Philippians 2:1-11 aloud together. Each group should have at least two different languages going at the same time!

When children finish reading the passage, ask:

● **How did it feel to hear so many different languages at once?**

● **How easy or difficult was it to understand the Scripture you were reading?**

Say: **I couldn't understand a word you were saying! I didn't know any of your languages, and they were all going on at once. Listen as I read the Scripture again in a language we can all understand.**

Reread the Scripture in English. Ask:

● **How is Jesus described in this Scripture?**

● **How did the people at the Tower of Babel differ from Jesus as he is described in this Scripture?**

Say: **God wants us to be humble, as Jesus was. Jesus could have bragged and boasted about being the Son of God, but instead he humbly carried out God's plan.**

Ask:

● **How can we live out this Scripture in our class?**

Post responses on a sheet of newsprint or a chalkboard to remind kids to serve each other with humility each time they come to class.

🖐 PHYSICAL

Supplies: Various "building" materials found around your church, such as books, plastic containers, blocks, erasers, or thick markers

Preparation: If you want to borrow supplies from other classrooms, make arrangements with the other teachers ahead of time.

Form groups of six. Have each group use "building" materials found in and around the church to build a structure that's six feet high and only touches the floor in three places. If children have trouble finding materials, suggest items such as books, hymnals, chalkboard or dry-erase board erasers, or thick markers. Supervise children as they gather their materials, and point out any items that are off-limits for this project.

As kids work together, point out instances of cooperation that are pleasing to God. When groups finish building their structures, have them discuss the following questions:

● **What was hard about working together on your structures? What was easy?**

● **How are your structures like the Tower of Babel? How are they different?**

Say: **Building these structures was a fun way to review our Bible story and to practice working together. What other ways can we work together when we come to this class?**

Take kids' suggestions and then say: **Those are great ideas! I know something else we can do together—pray. Let's pray together now.**

Close the activity by thanking God for your class and for the uniqueness of each person in it.

Logical

Supplies: Bibles, paper, pencils, and markers

Preparation: none

No one knows for sure what the Tower of Babel looked like. Genesis 11:1-9 only offers two clues: it was tall, and it was built with bricks and tar. But logical-mathematical thinkers will enjoy using these clues to imagine what the finished tower may have looked like.

Form pairs. Give each pair paper, pencils, markers, and a Bible. Have partners read Genesis 11:1-9 and then draw a picture together of the tower they envision. As kids work, encourage them to think about the following questions:

- **How many bricks would it take to build your tower?**
- **What equipment would you need to build your tower?**
- **How many people would it take to build your tower?**
- **How long would it take to complete your tower?**

After pairs are finished, bring them together and have a show and tell time for pairs to explain their towers to the group. Remember: There are no wrong answers. After pairs have all explained their towers, say: **Building these towers would have taken a lot of effort.** Ask:

- **Do you think God was pleased with the effort the people put into building the tower? Why or why not?**
- **What kind of effort would have pleased God?**
- **What kinds of efforts can we make that will please God?**

Remind kids to look for ways they can please God by working together for him this week.

Interpersonal

Supplies: A Bible, supplies needed to complete a twenty-minute service project of children's choosing, and snacks (optional)

Preparation: Gather supplies and make any necessary arrangements for one or more of the projects suggested below. If you want, prepare a snack for children to enjoy after they've completed their project.

Read aloud Philippians 2:1-4. Tell children that God is pleased when his people work together for good causes. Have your class work together to come up with a project they could complete in twenty minutes that would please God. For example, kids may decide to write an encouraging letter to the pastor, clean the church bathrooms, or wash car windows in the parking lot. Lead children in working to carry out their worthy cause.

After kids finish their project, invite them to share what they enjoyed most about working together for a worthy cause. Affirm kids for their work, and offer the snack you've prepared.

 **REFLECTIVE**

Supplies: Bibles

Preparation: none

Distribute Bibles, and help children find Psalm 139:23-24. Say: **The people who built the Tower of Babel were doing one thing right—working together. But instead of working together to glorify God, they worked pridefully to make a name for themselves. Like the people who built the Tower of Babel, sometimes we do the right things for the wrong reasons. But if we tell God about our wrong thoughts and reasons, he promises to forgive us. Listen to what the Bible says about that.**

Read aloud Psalm 139:23-24. Then have each child silently reread and think about these verses. Encourage children to ask God to search their hearts and reveal any wrong motives they may have. Encourage children to confess wrong motives to God and receive his forgiveness.

EXTRA! EXTRA! EXTRA! EXTRA! EXTRA!

- If you have access to a gymnasium or fellowship hall and floor mats, have kids work together to build a human pyramid.

- Have children work together to build a tower sandwich with layers of meat, cheese, bread, lettuce, and condiments. Then have them split the sandwich up and eat it.

- Have your lesson at the highest place in your church or town. Ask kids to think about whether anyone could ever really build a tower high enough to reach into the heavens.

- Read aloud Revelation 7:9-12. Have kids discuss these questions:

- **What is God's plan for all the different people in the world?**

- **How is this scene in heaven the same as or different from the scene at the Tower of Babel?**

EXTRA! EXTRA! EXTRA! EXTRA! EXTRA!

Sold Into Slavery

As they examine the remarkable events of Joseph's life, kids will discover that God has good plans for their lives.

 **PHYSICAL**

Supplies: Bibles, three grocery bags, a marker, and the story-bag contents listed below

Preparation: Before class, label three grocery bags "Bag 1," "Bag 2," and "Bag 3." On Bag 1, write the reference "Genesis 37:1-4, 12-36." On Bag 2, write the reference "Genesis 41:1-16, 25-43, 46-49, 53-57." On Bag 3, write the reference "Genesis 42:1-28; 43:1-15, 26-30; 45:1-9, 25-28." Place the following items in the bags:

Bag 1	Bag 2	Bag 3
● a sheep (could be a toy, a picture, or cotton balls glued to a sheet of paper) ● a multicolored shirt or coat (could be a photo or a drawing) ● money (could be play or real money)	● a cow (could be a toy, a photo, or a drawing) ● grain (could be unpopped popcorn, wheat, or flour) ● a toy ring ● a man's dress shirt	● a picture of a boy labeled Benjamin ● a crown ● a mask or a pair of glasses with a nose attached ● a box of facial tissue ● a piece of rope or twine ● a shopping bag ● grain (could be unpopped popcorn, wheat, or flour) ● money (could be play or real money) ● a can or jar of nuts

Form three groups. (A group can consist of one person.) Give each group a story bag. Have each group read the Scriptures written on its bag and use the items in the bag to create a skit to act out the Scriptures. Allow ten to fifteen minutes for preparation.

When kids have prepared their presentations, bring groups together and have them act out their stories for the whole group, beginning with the Bag 1 group. After the presentations, ask:
- **What did you learn about Joseph in this story?**
- **What did you learn about God?**

Say: **Even when things seemed really bad for Joseph, he never** stopped trusting God. And God never stopped looking out for Joseph. Although Joseph had to endure many troubles, God used those troubles to allow Joseph to help many people, including his own family. God had a good plan for Joseph's life, and he has good plans for our lives, too.

visual

Supplies: Bibles, large sheets of paper, pencils, markers or crayons, and tape or pins

Preparation: none

Explain to children that Joseph's older brothers committed a serious offense when they sold their little brother Joseph. If they had committed this crime today, they would be searched out and thrown into jail.

Say: **Let's make Wanted posters for each of Joseph's brothers. Read Genesis 49:3-21, and choose a brother to create a Wanted poster for. Let me know who you choose so we can be sure that every brother meets his just reward.**

Distribute Bibles and set out large sheets of paper, pencils, and markers or crayons. Have some children make more than one poster if necessary to make sure each of the brothers has a poster. Help children understand the components of a Wanted poster: a picture of the criminal, the word "Wanted" across the top, a brief description of the wanted person and the crime he's committed, and a promise of a reward.

When the posters are finished, hang them side by side on a wall or bulletin board in your room. Have kids take turns describing their posters. Then say: **Joseph's brothers did a terrible thing to Joseph, and they deserved to be punished. But even though Joseph was in a powerful position and could have punished them, he forgave them instead. God can help us forgive people who are mean to us just as he helped Joseph forgive his brothers.**

verbal

Supplies: Paper and pencils

Preparation: none

Form pairs, and distribute paper and pencils. Say: **During the time that Joseph was in slavery, he was wrongfully accused and thrown in prison. In Matthew 25, the Bible tells us that God is pleased when we do good things for people who are in prison. We weren't there when Joseph was in prison, but let's pretend that we're there now. Work with your partner to write a letter to encourage Joseph. Of course, we know that God took care of Joseph and helped him get out of prison, but Joseph didn't know that would happen. Think of what you'd say to Joseph to make him feel better.**

Give kids five to ten minutes to write their letters. Then ask for volunteers to read their letters to the group. After kids have read their letters, say: **Things couldn't have been much worse for Joseph. His brothers betrayed him, he'd been sold as a slave, and then he was unjustly thrown in prison because someone lied about him. But as your letters pointed out, God was with him all along. God is always with us, too. Let's thank him right now.**

Close this activity by inviting volunteers to say prayers of thanks for God's constant care.

♫ MUSICAL

Supplies: CD or cassette player and a recording of "Swing Low, Sweet Chariot" or another spiritual of your choice

Preparation: Practice singing "Swing Low, Sweet Chariot" so you can teach it to kids.

Say: **Joseph's brothers did a terrible thing by selling him into slavery. At one time in our own country's history, a similar terrible thing was done. Black people were made to be slaves. They were brought from their homeland in Africa and sold to people in America. Their lives were very hard, but, like Joseph, many of these people turned to God and trusted him to help them. Let's sing a song they sang to comfort themselves.**

Lead children in singing "Swing Low, Sweet Chariot" (or another spiritual of your choice). Then ask:

● **How do you think the people who sang this song felt?**
● **Where did they find comfort?**
● **How do you think Joseph felt when he was sold into slavery?**
● **How would you have felt if you were forced to leave your family and work as a slave for a total stranger?**
● **How were Joseph and the person who wrote this song similar?**

Say: **The Bible promises that we can trust God to work things out for the best—even when they seem to be the worst! God comforted Joseph, he comforted the slaves in America, and he'll comfort us today.**

⅜ LOGICAL

Supplies: Bibles, paper, pencils, and newsprint and a marker or a chalkboard and chalk

Preparation: If you have access to a computer with games installed, consider setting it up and showing kids a sample computer game. Write the following components on newsprint or a chalkboard.

- a final goal
- obstacles to prevent characters in the game from reaching the goal
- ways to earn points
- the number of "lives" a character has in one game
- traps to take away lives

Form groups of four. If possible, make sure at least one child in each group is familiar with computer games. Distribute Bibles, paper, and pencils. Tell kids that they're going to work to create computer games about Joseph. Have kids include the components written on the newsprint or chalkboard in their games.

Have kids match these components to Scripture as much as possible. For example, the goal of the game could be Joseph's freedom. Players could lose lives by falling into the pit or by being put in prison. Encourage kids to reread portions of the Bible story from Genesis 37:1–45:28 to get ideas for their game components. Have kids list their game components or draw sample game screens.

Allow ten to fifteen minutes for kids to create their games and then invite volunteers to describe their games to the group. After kids have described their games, say: **Joseph probably worried about losing his life or being trapped—not just in a game, but in real life. Fortunately, he knew that God was in control. If you find yourself feeling trapped this week, remember that God is in control of your life, too.**

Interpersonal

Supplies: A Bible

Preparation: none

Form pairs. Say: **Although Joseph may not have known it when he was sold into slavery, God was in control of his life. Later, Joseph realized that God had a purpose for everything that had happened to him. Listen to Joseph's words.**

Read aloud Genesis 45:4-8. Ask:

● **How does it make you feel to know that God has good things planned for you when you're going through bad things?**

Read aloud Romans 8:28. Ask:

● **How was this verse true for Joseph?**

● **How is this verse true for you?**

Say: **Partners, tell each other about a bad thing you've gone through or are going through. Then think of one way God could do something good through the bad thing your partner mentioned. For example, maybe your partner's parents got a divorce. God may want to use your partner to encourage other kids and help them if their parents ever divorce.**

Allow five minutes for partners to share and then encourage kids to pray together about the hard things they're going through.

Reflective

Supplies: none

Preparation: none

Say: **Joseph and his brothers didn't get along. Joseph was spoiled, and his brothers were jealous of him. Because Joseph and his brothers didn't deal with these problems, the problems became even bigger problems.**

Think about your relationships with your brothers and sisters. If you don't have brothers and sisters, think about your relationships with your friends. Ask God to show you any problems you may need to deal with or things you may need to ask forgiveness for.

Allow five minutes for kids to reflect and pray silently and then close by asking God to work in kids' relationships this week.

Extra! Extra! Extra! Extra! Extra!

● Conduct a "slave auction" to raise money for a mission. Have kids auction off blocks of time when they'll do housework, yardwork, or baby-sitting for church members. Donate the money kids earn to a local children's home or another mission. Afterward, have kids discuss the experience of being a slave.

● Have kids write letters of appreciation or apology to siblings.

● Arrange for kids to write letters of encouragement to children of local prison inmates.

Extra! Extra! Extra! Extra! Extra!

Free at Last

Kids will learn about God's deliverance as they discover how God led his people out of Egypt.

PHYSICAL

Supplies: none

Preparation: Read over the story, and prepare to lead children in doing the motions in parentheses.

Say: **A long time ago, God's people were forced to work in Egypt as slaves. The Egyptians made them work hard all day in the hot sun. But the people cried out to God, and God heard them. Let's do some motions as we hear about God leading his people out of slavery.**

Lead children in the motions in parentheses as you read the following story.

> **God said, "Moses, go and free my people from this slavery."** *(Pretend to break chains.)*
>
> **So Moses went to Pharoah and said, "Let my people go!"** *(Slide two steps sideways from left to right.)*
>
> **But Pharoah said "No!"** *(Place your hands on your hips, and shout "No!")*
>
> **So God sent ten plagues.**
>
> **Blood flowed in Egypt's rivers.** *(Hold your nose, and say "Egad!")*
>
> **So Moses went to Pharoah** *(slide two steps sideways),*
>
> **But Pharoah said "No!"** *(Place your hands on your hips, and shout "No!")*
>
> **Frogs hopped all over.** *(Hop like a frog.)*
>
> **So Moses went to Pharoah** *(slide two steps sideways),*
>
> **But Pharoah said "No!"** *(Place your hands on your hips, and shout "No!")*
>
> **Gnats swarmed.** *(Pretend to swat at gnats around your face.)*
>
> **So Moses went to Pharoah** *(slide two steps sideways),*
>
> **But Pharoah said "No!"** *(Place your hands on your hips, and shout "No!")*
>
> **Flies flew.** *(Pretend to swat at flies in the air.)*
>
> **So Moses went to Pharoah** *(slide two steps sideways),*
>
> **But Pharoah said "No!"** *(Place your hands on your hips, and shout "No!")*
>
> **Cows died.** *(Fall over and play dead.)*
>
> **So Moses went to Pharoah** *(slide two steps sideways),*
>
> **But Pharoah said "No!"** *(Place your hands on your hips, and shout "No!")*
>
> **People got big bumps on their bodies.** *(Point at pretend bumps on others' bodies.)*
>
> **So Moses went to Pharoah** *(slide two steps sideways),*
>
> **But Pharoah said "No!"** *(Place your hands on your hips, and shout "No!")*
>
> **Hail rained down from the sky.** *(Dodge imaginary hailstones.)*
>
> **So Moses went to Pharoah** *(slide two steps sideways),*
>
> **But Pharoah said "No!"** *(Place your hands on your hips, and shout "No!")*

Locusts filled the land. *(Pretend to fly around like a bug.)*

So Moses went to Pharaoh *(slide two steps sideways),*

But Pharoah said "No!" *(Place your hands on your hips, and shout "No!")*

Darkness covered Egypt. *(Cover your eyes, and pretend you can't see.)*

So Moses went to Pharoah *(slide two steps sideways),*

But Pharoah said "No!" *(Place your hands on your hips, and shout "No!")*

Then death came to the firstborn. *(Pretend to hold a baby, and make a sad face.)*

So Moses said, "Let my people go!" *(Stand still with your hands on your hips.)*

And finally, Pharoah said "Go!" *(Raise your arms up in the air, and shout "Go!")*

So Moses led God's people out of Egypt *(run to the other end of the room and have kids follow you),*

through the Red Sea *(lead kids in running single file down the middle of your room),*

and into the Promised Land. *(Sit down.)*

Invite kids to give themselves a hand for their participation in the story. You may want to allow a few moments of rest time before moving on to your next activity!

 # Visual

Supplies: Bibles, 4x6 cards, pencils, crayons or markers, tape or pins, and sample travel postcards (optional)

Preparation: none

Form four groups. Give each group a Bible, 4x6 cards, crayons or markers, and pencils. Assign each group one of the following Bible story sections:
- Exodus 3:1-21
- Exodus 7:8-24
- Exodus 8:1-32
- Exodus 12:31-42

Say: **Many of the events in our story took place in or around the land of Egypt. Pretend you're travelers in Egypt. Read your assigned part of the story and then design a picture postcard that shows what Egypt might have been like at that time. For example, you might draw an Egyptian pyramid covered with frogs or a cloud of bugs circling around Pharoah's head.**

Have groups read their assigned Scriptures and create several picture postcards that show Egypt during the plagues and the Exodus.

After the postcards are finished, invite kids to show them to the group.

If you're not using the Verbal activity, post kids' postcards on a wall or bulletin board.

If you'll be using the Verbal activity, continue: **During the plagues, Egypt was a strange and sometimes fascinating place. In our next activity, we'll write messages on our postcards to describe the events that happened there.**

Verbal

Supplies: Postcards from the Visual activity and pencils

Preparation: If you didn't do the Visual activity, you'll need to provide postcards.

Form pairs. (If you did the Visual activity, pair up kids within their groups.) Give each pair one or two postcards. Have pairs turn each postcard over and write a message to someone as though they were in Egypt during the events in the Bible story.

As kids work, suggest ideas they might include in their messages, such as "Wish you were here," "Having a wild time," or "Today we went to…" Remind kids to include information from the story in their messages.

When kids finish writing their messages, have pairs take turns showing and reading their cards to the rest of the class. After everyone has shared, say: **We don't have any postcards from the actual plagues and the Exodus. But we do have an even better record of what happened—the Bible. God's Word tells us that he delivered the Israelites from slavery in Egypt and that he can help deliver us from our troubles today.**

Musical

Supplies: Bibles, instrumental-music cassettes or CDs, and a cassette or CD player

Preparation: Select several instrumental-music cassettes or CDs. Any style of instrumental music will work for this activity—try to include a variety of styles.

Distribute Bibles, and have kids read Exodus 8. Have kids work in pairs or groups to select music and create motions for a frog, gnat, or fly dance. Explain that their motions can show the actions of the creatures or the responses of the Egyptians to the creatures that were attacking them. Encourage kids to use their imaginations and have fun with this activity!

When kids finish their dances, have them lead everyone in doing "The Frog," "The Gnat," and "The Fly." After you've tried all the dances, say: **There was certainly a whole lot of buzzing, ducking, swatting, and jumping going on in Egypt back then! I'm glad God delivered his people from the plagues.**

Logical

Supplies: A Bible, a Bible atlas, heavy-duty aluminum foil, masking tape, a marker, a large cookie sheet, an overhead projector, transparency sheets, scissors, prepared cookie dough, a rolling pin, an oven, and a tube of icing

Preparation: Photocopy a map of Egypt during Moses' time onto a transparency sheet. Set up an overhead projector where you can project the map onto a blank wall. Adjust the projector so the map is no larger than your cookie sheet. If your church doesn't have an oven, arrange to do this activity in someone's home.

Tell kids that you're going to make your own edible map of Egypt. Explain that everyone will have a job to help in making the map.

Assign the following jobs to individuals or groups of kids:

● Measure aluminum foil to fit the cookie sheet, and tape the foil to the wall. Place the foil so the projected map is on the foil.

● Use a marker to trace the map outline onto the foil.

● Remove the foil from the wall, and cut out the map outline. Place the foil cutout on the cookie sheet.

● Wash your hands. Place the cookie dough on the foil cutout. Roll out the dough evenly.

● Cut the dough so it just covers the foil outline.

Bake the cookie according to recipe instructions. While the cookie bakes, read Exodus 11:1–12:50. Ask:

● **How do you think the Israelites felt during the Passover as they waited to see if God would protect their firstborn sons?**

● **Tell about a time God protected you when you were afraid.**

After you take the cookie out of the oven, help kids use a Bible atlas to determine the route the Israelites followed as they left Egypt. When the cookie map is cool enough to touch, have kids draw the route on the map using a tube of icing.

Say: **The Israelites enjoyed a special meal together to celebrate God's deliverance. Before we eat our special cookie map, let's thank God for delivering us from scary situations.**

Invite a volunteer to pray and then enjoy the cookie together!

InterPersonal

Supplies: none

Preparation: none

Form pairs. Say: **The Israelites were delivered from their slavery in Egypt. To be delivered means to be removed from a problem or a troubling situation. Turn to your partner and tell him or her about something that you need deliverance from. It could be a problem at home, a temptation you've had, or an attitude you can't seem to change.**

After five minutes, say: **Let's ask God to deliver our friends from the problems they're facing. Take a couple of minutes to pray for each other and ask God for deliverance.**

Allow a few minutes for kids to pray together and then close by thanking God for hearing kids' prayers.

Reflective

Supplies: Photocopies of the "Light of Deliverance" handout, crayons or markers, scissors, glue, and pieces of lightweight cardboard (such as poster board or file folders)

Preparation: Photocopy the "Light of Deliverance" handout (p. 35). You'll need one handout for each child.

Say: **God spoke to Moses through a burning bush. The bright, hot fire got Moses' attention, but Moses was still afraid to obey God. He had all kinds of excuses why he wasn't the best choice to deliver God's people from Egypt. Sometimes we have excuses that keep us from obeying God fully too. Our excuses might be things such as "I'm too busy," "I'm not talented enough," or "My parents would never let me."**

Think about what excuse keeps you from obeying God. We're going to write encouraging messages on light-switch plate covers that will remind us of God's deliverance. Every time we turn on the lights in our

bedrooms, we'll be reminded to put our excuses aside and trust in God.

Set out crayons or markers, scissors, glue, and cardboard. Give each child a "Light of Deliverance" handout. Have children decorate the light-switch plate covers on their handouts. Then have them write encouraging messages on the light-switch plate covers that will remind them to obey God fully. These messages might be things such as "I'm not afraid to follow God" or "I will trust in God's plan for me."

Have kids cut out their finished covers and glue them to cardboard. Then have kids trim the cardboard to match. Encourage kids to hang their light-switch plate covers in their rooms at home.

EXTRA! EXTRA! Extra! Extra! Extra!

● Have kids create a "Ten Plagues" museum. Each plague could have its own exhibit. For example, for the plague of frogs, you might see how many frogs your kids can bring in and display in an aquarium. Or if you're in an urban setting, have kids create a "frog feely" box. What would all those frogs have felt like? Maybe green grapes and syrup mixed together! Let kids' imaginations go wild. Then invite other classes to visit your museum.

● Remind kids that Moses lacked confidence to do what God wanted. It was only as he grew in God-confidence that he was able to carry out God's will. Form pairs, and have partners tell each other about areas where they need God-confidence in their own lives.

● Children who learn well through music enjoy listening to music as they work. Even the presence of music helps them learn more. As children work on any of the other activities, play music in the background. Music with a triumphant theme such as the hymn "Crown Him With Many Crowns" or the theme songs from the movies *Rocky* or *Chariots of Fire* will best convey the victorious theme of this Bible story.

EXTRA! EXTRA! EXTRA! EXTRA! EXTRA!

LIGHT OF DELIVERANCE

Decorate the light-switch plate cover. Then write on it one encouraging message that will remind you to trust in God's deliverance.

Cut this out.

Let Freedom Ring

Kids will celebrate God's power as they learn how God parted the Red Sea for the Israelites.

✋ PHYSICAL

Supplies: A Bible

Preparation: None. If possible, arrange to do this activity outdoors or in a large room such as a gymnasium or a fellowship hall.

Read aloud Exodus 14:13-31. Say: **When Moses raised his hands, God opened the Red Sea for the Israelites to cross through. We're going to play a game in which a pretend Moses drops his hands every now and then.**

Play this game like Red Light, Green Light. Choose someone to be "Moses." Have Moses stand at one end of the room, and have the other children stand at the other end. Clear any furniture or other obstacles out of the way.

When Moses raises his or her hands, the other children may walk toward him or her. When Moses lowers his or her hands, the children must stop. Anyone who doesn't stop immediately must go back to the start. Play until someone reaches Moses. That person then becomes Moses. Play the game several times, as time allows.

After the game, ask:

● **How did you feel as Moses' hands dropped?**

● **How do you think the Israelites felt as they passed through the Red Sea?**

● **How quickly do you think the Israelites walked?**

● **If you had been an Israelite and experienced this, what would you tell your grandchildren about this experience when you were old?**

Say: **It must have been amazing to see God's powerful wind blowing the sea apart and then to walk between the walls of sea water. Our God is truly an awesome, powerful God!**

👁 VISUAL

Supplies: A Bible, large squares of light-colored felt, permanent markers, and dowels (optional)

Preparation: Cut felt into large squares for kids to use as banners. If you want to have kids mount their banners on dowels, you'll need to purchase two dowels for each child.

Say: **After 430 years of slavery in Egypt, the Israelites were set free.** Ask:

● **How do you think the Israelites felt to be free after many years of being slaves?**

● **How would you have felt?**

Give kids large felt squares and permanent markers. Have each child create a banner that celebrates the freedom the Israelites enjoyed. After kids finish their banners, read aloud John 8:32. Then have a parade with the banners through the halls of your church to celebrate the freedom God gives.

VERBAL

Supplies: Photocopies of "The Red Sea Zone" handout, scissors, glue, sturdy paper (such as card stock or file folders), paper fasteners, paper, pencils, construction paper (optional), and crayons or markers (optional)

Preparation: Photocopy "The Red Sea Zone" handout (p. 40). You'll need one copy for every four children. Cut out the spinner arrow at the bottom of each handout, and mount it on sturdy paper such as card stock. Use a paper fastener to attach the spinner to the center of each picture.

Form groups of four. Give each group a copy of "The Red Sea Zone" handout with a spinner attached. Have children in each group take turns spinning the spinner. Once the spinner stops, have children make up a story about what it would've been like to observe the events of the Bible story from the spot where the spinner landed.

For example, someone may say, "I was fishing at the Red Sea when God parted the waters. I couldn't believe my eyes. Fish were flopping everywhere. Hundreds of people came rushing through the parted waters on dry land..."

Let each group spin its spinner several times. Then have groups share their stories with the class. Have kids in each group help each other choose a favorite story to write down and share with others. Provide paper and pencils for kids to write their stories. If you want, provide construction paper and crayons or markers and let kids design covers and turn their stories into books.

End with groups reading their stories for one another. Then say: **Those are great stories. It's fun to imagine what it would have been like to witness an exciting Bible story like this one. The Bible is full of exciting stories about how God helped his people in Bible times. God helps us today, too!**

MUSICAL

Supplies: A Bible, paper plates, crepe paper streamers, markers, dried beans, and a stapler

Preparation: none

Say: **After God led his people through the Red Sea, Moses and his sister, Miriam, sang a beautiful song of praise. We're going to make beautiful music to their song with tambourines that we create.**

Distribute paper plates, crepe paper streamers, and markers. Have each child use the markers to draw colorful pictures on the bottoms of two plates.

When kids finish drawing, have each child pour a couple handfuls of dried beans onto one of his or her plates. Then have each child tear off several two-foot crepe paper streamers and lay them on his or her plate. Show kids how to place their two plates together—with plate bottoms out—and staple at quarter-inch intervals around the edges of the plates so no beans fall out.

Demonstrate how to use a tambourine. Show kids how to shake their tambourines in one of their hands and tap the tambourines gently with their other hands. Kids can dance around as they play their tambourines.

Read aloud Exodus 15:1-18. Kids can shake their tambourines as you read. Stop every one or two lines to let children emphasize the song with their tambourines.

If your kids are really musical, encourage them to put Moses' song to music. They can make up their own tune or put the words to a well-known tune such as "Twinkle, Twinkle, Little Star" or "Row, Row, Row Your Boat."

Logical

Supplies: Two boxes, paper, and pencils

Preparation: none

Form two groups. Tell kids that they're going to pretend that they were there when God set the Israelites free. Ask:

● **What things would you have taken with you as you left Egypt?**

● **What things would've been important to you during your journey?**

Say: **A time capsule is something people make to store items that are typical of their lives. They put the time capsule away to be opened years later. Their hope is that whoever opens the time capsule will see what their lives were like and will learn about them.**

Let's make a time capsule and fill it with things that the Israelites may have put in a time capsule as God set them free. What kinds of things might they have put in their time capsule?

Take a few responses, then give each group a box, paper, and pencils. Say: **Work with your group to create an Exodus time capsule. You can draw pictures or write about the items the Israelites may have put in their time capsule. Remember to think about everyday items and faith-related items. Maybe these people had a favorite Bible verse that strengthened them. Or maybe they had a prayer that they said at mealtime. Use your imaginations and your logical thinking. Make sure all your items would be true to that time. I don't want to see any televisions in those boxes!**

Allow ten to fifteen minutes for kids to work on their time capsules. Once the time capsules are finished, have groups show each other what they've made. Then seal the time capsules. Say: **We'll put these away for next year's class. After they make their own time capsules, we'll let them open these to see what you came up with.**

(Note: If you've used this activity with classes in previous years, open up the previous group's time capsules and explore what they made.)

Interpersonal

Supplies: Photocopies of the "Passport" handout and pencils

Preparation: Photocopy and cut apart the "Passport" handout (p. 41). You'll need one copy for each child.

Form pairs. Say: **When the Israelites left Egypt, they didn't have to worry about tickets or travel documents. If we go to another country today, we are required by law to have a legal identification document called a passport.**

Ask:

● **How many of you already have passports?**

● **Who can tell us what a passport looks like?**

Hold up a copy of the "Passport" handout. Say: **A passport has a photograph of the person, identifying information, and stamps to show where that person has traveled. We're going to make passports for our partners—with a different twist. For identifying information, we're going to list all the great things about our partners so the "officials" in any country will be able to identify our friends. For example, you might write "great singer, good friend, silly sense of humor, gorgeous**

blonde hair." Keep your descriptions positive.

Give each child a "Passport" handout. When partners finish writing descriptions on each other's passports, have them trade and read the affirming statements.

✥ Reflective

Supplies: Photocopies of the "Free Indeed" coupon

Preparation: Photocopy and cut apart the "Free Indeed" coupons (p. 41). You'll need one coupon for each child.

Give each child a "Free Indeed" coupon. Say: **God set the Israelites free from bondage. Jesus set us free from the bondage of sin when he died for us on the cross. Think about one thing that Jesus has set you free from that you're grateful for. It may be that Jesus has freed you from a future of pain or from a present-day problem. Think about what you've been set free from, and write it on your "Free Indeed" coupon.**

Allow a few moments for kids to fill in their coupons and reflect on the freedom God has given them. Then close by thanking God for the freedom he has given us in Christ.

Extra! Extra! Extra! Extra! Extra!

● Have children create their own time capsules to commemorate the wonderful things that God has done for them. Kids could include tape-recorded messages, writings, or objects. Have them date their time capsules and write a date that they or someone else can open them.

● Have children paint a mural on a wall in your room to tell the story of God delivering the Israelites. If you can't get permission to paint on a real wall, cover your wall with paper first.

● Create a fun play with overhead transparencies by using the "Moses and the Exodus" skit in *Big Action Bible Skits* (available from Group Publishing.)

EXTRA! EXTRA! EXTRA! EXTRA! EXTRA!

THE RED SEA ZONE

Passport

PASSPORT

PASSPORT OFFICIAL VISA

COUPON

FREE INDEED

Jesus, thank you for freeing me from _____

_____

_____

Tumbling Down

Kids will discover the good results that come from obeying God as they hear about how Joshua obeyed God's directions to bring down the walls of Jericho.

Logical

Supplies: A Bible, paper, and pencils

Preparation: none

Don't tell kids anything about today's Bible story yet. In an excited tone of voice, say: **We need to plan a big strategy for a battle. Our army has to get into a city, but there are walls all around it. What can we do?**

Form groups of three, and give each group paper and pencils. Tell groups to come up with a plan to get into the city. After about five minutes, ask groups to report their strategies.

After all the reports, say: **The Bible tells us about a man named Joshua who faced the same dilemma. Listen to what God told him to do.**

Read aloud Joshua 6:2-20. Then ask:
● **How does God's strategy compare to ours?**
● **If God told you to do what he told Joshua to do, what would you think? What would you do?**
● **How easy or difficult is it to do the things God tells you to do through his Word?**

Say: **Joshua obeyed God even though people may have laughed at him. God wants us to obey him no matter what.**

Visual

Supplies: Bibles and modeling dough

Preparation: Mark Joshua 6:2-20 in several Bibles.

Form two groups. Set out modeling dough and Bibles with Joshua 6:2-20 marked. Have one group work together to create a modeling-dough version of Jericho. Have the other group create Joshua and his army marching around Jericho out of modeling dough. Encourage kids to read the biblical account to make sure they include all the parts of the story in their modeling-dough version.

When kids finish their modeling-dough creations, have the Joshua group "march" their creations around the modeling-dough Jericho. Let the Jericho group knock down their own walls.

Say: **It was easy to knock down our modeling-dough walls. But the real Jericho had high stone walls—only God could knock them down. Because Joshua obeyed God's instructions, good things happened—God knocked down the walls and led his people to victory. Good things happen when we obey God, too.**

Verbal

Supplies: Pencils, paper, and a camcorder (optional)

Preparation: If possible, arrange to borrow a camcorder from someone in your church so you can videotape kids' interviews.

Form pairs. Have the partner in each pair who looks most like a news reporter be the reporter. Have the other partner in each pair pretend to have been there when the walls of Jericho came down. This person can be one of the marchers, Joshua himself, or one of the people in Jericho. Explain that in a few minutes, the reporters will interview the firsthand observers about their experiences at Jericho.

Have all the reporters meet in one corner of your room to brainstorm questions they'll ask in their interviews. Provide pencils and paper for reporters to jot down ideas. Have this group agree on the top three questions.

While the reporters are meeting, have the firsthand observers meet in another corner to discuss what it might've been like to be there when the walls came tumbling down.

Bring partners back together, and have reporters conduct their interviews one at a time. After all the interviews, say: **Thank you, reporters and observers! What an exciting story. Tune in next time for another chapter of "Dateline Jericho."**

EXTRA! EXTRA! EXTRA! EXTRA! EXTRA!

For fun, bring a camcorder and videotape all the interviews. Then let kids take turns taking the video home to show their families.

EXTRA! EXTRA! EXTRA! EXTRA! EXTRA!

 ## MUSICAL

Supplies: CD or cassette recording of "Joshua Fought the Battle of Jericho" (optional) and a CD or cassette player (optional)

Preparation: Practice singing "Joshua Fought the Battle of Jericho" so you can teach it to your class. If you want, make arrangements for children to teach the song to other classes.

Lead children in singing the spiritual "Joshua Fought the Battle of Jericho." Then have children work together in groups of three to create motions for the song. After about ten minutes, have each group present its version of the song to the rest of the class. For fun, have trios go to different classes and teach them the song—complete with motions.

 ## PHYSICAL

Supplies: none

Preparation: none

Say: **The walls of Jericho came tumbling down when Joshua obeyed God. Let's see if we can build a wall with our bodies that no one can tear down. We'll need two people who'll volunteer to topple our walls over.**
Choose two volunteers and then have the rest of the group build a structure with their bodies that no assailant can tear down. Kids might link arms and stand strong, build a pyramid, or huddle together in a tight clump.

After the structure is built, give the two "topplers" three tries to tear it down. Make sure the topplers know not to use pain-inflicting methods such as pinching or kicking. Then ask:

- **Builders, how did you feel as you built your structure?**
- **Topplers, how did you feel as you tried to knock over the structure?**
- **Builders and topplers, how did you feel as the topplers were** (or were not) **successful?**
- **How do you think the people of Jericho felt when their walls came tumbling down?**
- **How do you think Joshua and his men felt?**

Say: **We may or may not be able to build a structure that can't be torn down, but we know that God can do anything. God can do whatever he tells us he'll do. We have a mighty God.**

Close by praying that kids will be able to do what God wants them to do this week.

 INTERPERSONAL

Supplies: Index cards, pencils, and tape

Preparation: Write each child's name on three separate index cards. Be sure to be prepared with extra index cards in case you have visitors.

Say: **We celebrate Joshua's faith today because he believed God and obeyed. Let's celebrate each other's faith by creating a wall of remembrance.**

Shuffle and distribute the cards. Give each child a pencil and three cards with different names on them. Say: **You have cards with people's names on them. Write on each person's card one way you've seen that person demonstrate faith or obey God. Keep your comments positive.**

Allow at least five minutes for kids to write on each other's cards. When the cards are finished, have kids tape them to the wall as though they're bricks. Use these "bricks" to create a "wall" of remembrance. Give kids time to read all the great things others said about their faith and obedience.

REFLECTIVE

Supplies: A Bible, index cards, and pencils

Preparation: none

Give each child an index card and a pencil. Read aloud Hebrews 11:1-2, 30. Say: **Joshua is remembered for being a man of faith. Other people in the Bible are also remembered for their faith, such as Abraham, Noah, and King David. When a person dies, others like to talk about what they'll remember most about that person, such as his or her kindness, his or her sense of humor, or his or her generosity. Think about what you'd like to be remembered for. Write that characteristic on your card.**

Allow a few moments for kids to write on their cards and then close with a prayer similar to this one: "Dear God, we want to be remembered for our faith and trust in you. Help us to do what you want us to do. In Jesus' name, amen."

EXTRA! EXTRA! EXTRA! EXTRA! EXTRA!

● Form groups of six to eight. Have groups use newspaper to build free-standing structures large enough to contain all their group members.

● In groups of three, have kids talk about difficult obstacles they're facing. After a child shares an obstacle, have other kids think of wild "It Could Happen" solutions. For example, if a child talks about not having any Christian friends at school, the other kids might say: "What if Jesus visited your school? Then all the kids would believe in him, and you wouldn't be alone anymore" or "What if you stand up at an assembly and announce that you love Jesus? You could ask anyone who loves Jesus to stand with you. Maybe hundreds of kids would stand."

   After each child has had a turn, ask: **How crazy were the solutions people thought of?**

   Say: **Think of one seemingly crazy solution and think of how God could make a miracle for you using that solution. You may need to revise the solution a bit.** For example, tell kids that instead of announcing their love for Jesus in an assembly, they might begin by telling a few kids in their class about their love for Jesus. Pretty soon, God will reveal other kids that love him too.

● Create a fun play with overhead transparencies by using "The Fall of Jericho" skit in *Big Action Bible Skits* (available from Group Publishing).

EXTRA! EXTRA! EXTRA! EXTRA! EXTRA!

Sapped Strength

As they hear how Samson lost his strength, kids will discover the disastrous consequences that can result from disobeying God.

Visual

📖 **Supplies**: A broom, a string mop, paper, markers, scissors, and tape

Preparation: Draw three faces on paper, two female and one male. Make one of the female faces devious looking. Tape the female faces to the broom, as shown in the margin. Tape the male face to one side of the mop, as shown in the margin.

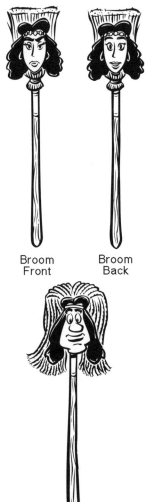

Broom Front   Broom Back

Mop

SAMSON'S STORY

Say: **I'd like to introduce you to a man named Samson. Say hello to Samson.** (Hold up the mop.) **Samson was promised to God as a Nazirite since before his birth. That meant he was never supposed to drink any wine or cut his hair.** (Stroke the mop's strings.) **Samson obeyed, and God made Samson the strongest man ever.**

But one day, Samson met Delilah. (Hold up the broom.) **Samson fell head over heels in love with Delilah.** (Dip the mop's strings to the floor. Then have the broom "kiss" the mop.) **Samson didn't know that Delilah was two-faced.** (Turn the broom around, and show the other face.) **Delilah was working for the Philistine army. The Philistine army was tired of Samson being stronger than all of them put together. So they asked Delilah** (hold the broom forward) **to discover the secret of Samson's strength.**

Delilah begged Samson to tell her his secret for strength. (Say "Please, please, please!" as you "jump" the broom up and down.) **Samson finally told Delilah that if she cut his hair** (stroke the mop's strings), **he would be as weak as a mop. So when Samson fell asleep** (lay the mop down on a table), **Delilah had his hair cut.** (Have children help cut the strings of the mop.)

Sure enough, Samson became so weak that the Philistines captured him, blinded him, and imprisoned him. (Put the mop in a corner of your room.) **But Samson's hair grew back, his strength returned, and God helped him defeat the Philistines.** (Bring the mop back to the center of the room.)

Have the broom and the mop take a bow. Then give each child a string from the mop to help them remember the story. Say: **Just as God used Samson for good things when Samson obeyed God, God can use us for good when we obey him. Tie your string around your finger to remind you to obey God this week.**

VERBAL

Supplies: A Bible and newsprint and a marker or a chalkboard and chalk

Preparation: none

Read Judges 13:2-14, 24-25 and Judges 16:21 aloud. Ask:
- **How do you think Samson felt when he was in jail?**
- **What do you think he thought about?**

Say: **Let's pretend we're Samson in jail. We'll write a letter to Samson's parents telling them about our thoughts and feelings and about what it's like to be in jail.**

Have children call out things Samson might write in a letter to his parents. They might suggest ideas such as "I never should have listened to Delilah" or "It's really drafty here in jail—especially since I have no hair." Write children's responses on a large sheet of newsprint or a chalkboard.

When you've finished the letter, invite a volunteer to read the entire letter aloud. Then say: **Samson must have been miserable in prison. He could have avoided that misery by obeying God and turning away from Delilah's temptation. Giving in to temptation always leads to trouble. So the next time you're tempted to disobey God, remember what happened to Samson!**

MUSICAL

Supplies: A CD or cassette player and a CD or cassette of "Jesus Loves Me" or another simple, familiar praise song

Preparation: Select the song you'll use, and practice singing it.

Say: **God gave Samson great strength in his body, and Samson used that strength to glorify God. We don't have Samson's strength, but we can still use our bodies to glorify God. Let's sing a favorite praise song. Instead of using our singing voices, we'll see how many different sounds our bodies can make.**

Tell kids to avoid bodily function sounds. Encourage them to think of all the sounds their bodies can make, such as clapping, stomping, smacking, tongue-clicking, finger-snapping, and hand-rubbing.

After kids have chosen the sounds they'll use, lead them in "Jesus Loves Me" or another familiar praise song.

LOGICAL

Supplies: Bibles, pencils, and six photocopies of the "Character Report Card" handout

Preparation: Photocopy the "Character Report Card" handout (p. 50).

Ask:
- **How many of you get report cards in school?**
- **What information is included on a report card?**
- **What's the purpose of report cards?**

Form three groups.

Say: **Report cards are one way teachers let you and your families know how you're doing in school. Just for fun, today we're going to** make report cards for the people in our Bible story. But instead of reporting on school subjects, we'll report on how well the people in the story did with some important character qualities.

Form three groups. Give each group pencils, Bibles, and two Character Report Cards.

Say: **Read Judges 16:4-30. Then, based on what you read, make one report card for Delilah and one for Samson. Judge how well you think each person did in each character-quality section.** Encourage kids to use letter grades similar to those that they receive in school.

After ten minutes, have groups report about their report cards to the rest of the class. Average the three groups' grades to give Samson and Delilah a class grade.

After you announce the grades (they'll probably be low!), say: **Samson and Delilah had a lot to learn about honesty, obedience to God, loyalty, and moral purity. Think about those four character qualities this week. Take a few moments during the week to grade yourself and see how your character-quality report card might turn out!**

PHYSICAL

Supplies: A blindfold

Preparation: Clear the room of furniture or other obstacles.

Say: **When Samson was blinded and in prison, his hair grew back and his strength returned. Samson died when he caused a giant building to fall down on his enemies and himself. We're going to play a game called Blind Samson's Tag to remind us of what happened to Samson.**

Choose one person to be "Samson." Blindfold Samson. Have the other kids walk (not run) around the room as Samson tries to tag them. When Samson says "Samson," the other kids must respond by saying "Delilah." If anyone is tagged, that person becomes Samson.

Play for five minutes. When you're ready to stop playing, call out: **The building's falling! Everybody down!**

INTERPERSONAL

Supplies: Bibles, paper, pencils, newsprint and a marker or a chalkboard and chalk

Preparation: none

Form pairs. Say: **Samson needed help avoiding disaster. God had given him only two rules: he could never drink wine and he could never cut his hair. Samson did not listen to God so he met with disaster.**

Maybe Samson needed more rules to help him avoid disaster. Work with a partner to come up with three guidelines to help Samson be successful. For example, you may want to say "Always listen to God" or "Don't trust Delilah."

Distribute paper, pencils, and Bibles. Encourage kids to refer to the Bible story in Judges 16:4-30 if they need help coming up with their guidelines.

After five minutes, ask pairs to report their guidelines to the rest of the class. Write each guideline on a sheet of newsprint or a chalkboard. As you write each guideline, have other pairs give a thumbs-up signal if they think the guideline is in line with God's Word and a thumbs-down signal if they think the guideline is not in line with God's Word.

After you've written all the guidelines, say: **Samson got into trouble when he didn't listen to God. Maybe if he'd had all these great guidelines to help him, he would have remembered to do things God's way. It's always a good idea to listen to God and to look to the Bible for help when we're in trouble. Remember to do that this week.**

ReFlective

Supplies: Paper and pencils

Preparation: none

Distribute paper and pencils. Say: **If you could think of one guideline for your life that would help you avoid disaster, what would it be? For example, you might choose a guideline such as "Put God first in everything" or "It doesn't pay to disobey." Think of a guideline for yourself that will help you avoid disaster. When you've decided on a guideline, write it down.**

Allow a few minutes for kids to reflect and create their own guidelines. Encourage them to pray and ask God to help them avoid disaster this week by remembering their guidelines.

Extra! Extra! Extra! Extra! Extra!

● Create a fun play with overhead transparencies by using the "Samson and Delilah" skit in *Big Action Bible Skits* (available from Group Publishing).

● Have kids create a puppet play about an aspect of Samson's life to present to younger children. Ask: **What character qualities really make a person strong?**

List the qualities kids mention. Ask kids to name people in your class who display those qualities. Then have kids think of people outside of your class who display those qualities, such as friends, family members, or church members. Encourage children to call the people they've thought of this week to tell them that they admire their strength of character.

Extra! Extra! Extra! Extra! Extra!

CHARACTER REPORT CARD

Read Judges 16:4-30 and then fill in the report card for either Samson or Delilah.

Character Quality	Grade	Explanation
Honesty		
Obedience to God		
Loyalty		
Moral Purity		

A Woman of Excellence

Verbal

Supplies: A simple costume for a Bible character and sandals

Preparation: Practice the following script so you can perform it without any notes.

Act the part of a servant throughout this activity. As kids arrive, treat them as guests in your master's house. Offer to remove their shoes, provide chairs for them to sit on, or even offer simple refreshments. When everyone has arrived, begin your story.

Kids will learn the true meaning of loyalty as they hear about Ruth's loyalty to her mother-in-law Naomi.

RUTH and BOAZ: A LOVE STORY

Hi. My name is Joanna, and I am a servant in the house of Boaz. You'll never believe the love story I have to tell you.

You see, a woman named Ruth came to our threshing floor and lay down at the feet of my master when he was sleeping. Whoa! When he awoke and saw her, was he ever surprised!

Boaz had had his eye on Ruth for weeks. Everyone knew that Ruth was an excellent woman. Why, when her husband died in Moab, she didn't abandon Naomi, her mother-in-law. Ruth came back with Naomi to Bethlehem.

With no husband to take care of her, Ruth basically had to beg to get enough food for herself and Naomi to eat. She took the leftover grain from our fields. Boaz had compassion on her. He let her take as much grain as she needed, and he told us not to give her a hard time or make fun of her.

I could tell just by watching him that he was falling in love with Ruth. Well, when Boaz found Ruth lying at his feet, he told her he wanted to marry her. And he did marry her!

They got married, and they had a precious baby boy named Obed. Obed grew up and had children of his own. One of Obed's grandchildren was King David!

What a love story. What a happy ending. Ruth and Boaz loved each other, Naomi, their precious baby, and their God!

After you tell the story, ask:
● **What do you admire most about Ruth's story?**
● **Ruth was loyal to Naomi even when it was difficult. When is it difficult for you to be loyal to friends or family members?**
Say: **It wasn't easy for Ruth to take care of Naomi. She had to work hard every day to gather grain so she and Naomi would have enough to eat. She could have abandoned Naomi and just looked out**

for herself. But she didn't, and God honored her for her loyalty. God will honor our loyalty, too.

Visual

Supplies: Bibles, popped popcorn, glue, crayons or markers, light-colored construction paper, and tape or pins

Preparation: Pop several batches of popcorn.

Say: **Ruth worked in the fields. She picked up the grain the workers dropped or missed. Today we're going to use grain—popcorn—to create things from Ruth's story. You can create any of the parts of our Bible story. You may want to refer to Ruth 1:1–4:22 to help you remember parts of the story.**

Distribute Bibles, popped popcorn, glue, crayons or markers, and construction paper. Have kids draw parts of the story on their construction paper and then glue popcorn in appropriate places. For example, kids might use popcorn to fill a field with grain, clump pieces of popcorn together to create clothing on people they've drawn, or use popcorn for hair and facial features on close-ups of Ruth's face.

When kids finish, have them describe their creations to the class. Post the creations on a wall or a bulletin board to remind kids of Ruth's inspiring story.

Musical

Supplies: A Bible, various music CDs or cassettes, a CD or cassette player, paper, and pencils. If possible, provide several CD or cassette players.

Preparation: Select the music kids will choose from. If you want, limit your selections to typical wedding music (your church may have samples). Or provide all kinds of music, and let kids choose.

Form groups of three. Read the story of Boaz and Ruth's wedding aloud from Ruth 4:1-12. Then ask:

● **What kind of music do you think Boaz and Ruth had for their wedding?**

Say: **Now imagine that Boaz and Ruth's wedding took place today. What kind of music would they have? What songs do you think they would choose for a soloist to sing? Come up with a list of wedding music that you'd recommend for Boaz and Ruth's wedding.**

Set out paper, pencils, musical selections, and CD or cassette player(s). If a group is having trouble getting started, have the kids in that group join another group that seems to be coming up with a lot of ideas. Allow ten minutes for groups to select their music and then have groups read aloud their lists and tell why they chose those songs.

Close by saying: **What a beautiful wedding Boaz and Ruth would have had with all that music! Their wedding was the start of a beautiful relationship. Boaz and Ruth's son, Obed, was the grandfather of King David. Jesus' earthly father, Joseph, was also one of Boaz and Ruth's descendants.**

LOGiCAL

Supplies: Bibles, newsprint, and markers

Preparation: none

Read aloud Isaiah 9:6-7 and Luke 1:30-33. Distribute Bibles and markers. On a sheet of newsprint, have kids chart the lineage of Christ as recorded in Matthew 1:1-17. Afterward, ask:
- **Where is Ruth in this chart?**
- **Why was it important that Ruth was able to have a child?**
- **What would've happened if Ruth hadn't married Boaz and had a child? Would Jesus have been in the line of David as it was prophesied?**

Say: **Isaiah's prophecy and all of the other Old Testament prophecies about Jesus came true. How valuable would God's Word be if even just this one prophecy did not come true?**

Say: **All of God's promises are true. We know that Jesus is the Savior God promised because Jesus fulfills all of God's promises about him.**

Close by having each child complete the following sentence: "I know Jesus is God's Son because…"

PHYSiCAL

Supplies: Cotton balls, two rolls of masking tape, and two paper bags

Preparation: Spread cotton balls on the floor in a designated section of your room.

Say: **Ruth had to glean in the fields to find food for herself and Naomi. That meant that Ruth was looking for any grain that got left behind or spilled as the workers harvested the food for people to eat. Let's have a gleaning relay to see what it might've been like to glean in the fields.**

Have kids form two lines at one end of the room, opposite the area where you've spread the cotton balls. Each line is a team. Give each team a paper bag.

Give the first person in each line a roll of masking tape. Have that person tear off a piece of masking tape and wrap it around his or her hands with the sticky side out. Then have the first person hand the tape to the next person, who will do the same thing. Meanwhile, have the first person run to the cotton balls and take one chance to reach down and get as many cotton balls as possible to stick to his or her taped hands. The first person must then run back to the line and deposit the cotton balls in the paper bag. He or she may need teammates' help to do this.

Once the first person is back, the second person can take a turn "gleaning" the cotton balls. Continue until everyone has had a turn. Then count the cotton balls in each bag to see which team gleaned the most.

Say: **It was hard work for Ruth to glean in the fields. Yet she continued to do it in order to care for herself and her mother-in-law, Naomi. Ruth went out of her way to be kind. Take a cotton ball with you as a reminder to go out of your way to do something kind for a friend or a family member this week.**

InterPersonal

Supplies: Pencils, scrap paper, markers and other craft supplies, sturdy paper such as card stock, and a bag or bowl

Preparation: none

Say: **Ruth was an incredible woman. She was loyal to her mother-in-law, she worked hard, and she was a good wife to Boaz. I'd say she deserved an award. I think everyone in this class is incredible too. You all deserve awards!**

Distribute pencils and scrap paper, and have each child write his or her name on a piece of paper. Collect the names and put them in a bag or bowl. Have each child draw a name and return it only if he or she gets his or her own name. Then give children all kinds of craft supplies and sturdy paper. (If you can get them, unfinished wooden plaques from a craft-supply store would work well. You may want to use tempera paint instead of markers on these.)

Have each child create an award for the person whose name he or she drew. For example, kids may give awards for "The Kindest Person on Earth" or "The Most Likely to Pray About Problems."

When kids finish creating their awards, have an awards ceremony for kids to deliver and explain their awards. Close by giving everyone a big round of applause!

 Reflective

Supplies: none

Preparation: none

Say: **Ruth was an important part of Christ's heritage. She was a great-great-great-great-great—and more greats—grandmother to Jesus. God used her and many other people to fulfill the prophecy that Jesus would be born in King David's family.**

God also wants to use us to make sure that Jesus' family continues. We can continue Jesus' family by leading others into the family of God. Think about one way you can share your faith this week that could help someone follow Jesus.

Allow a few moments for kids to think and then pray and ask God to help children be faithful in continuing Jesus' family line.

Extra! Extra! Extra! Extra! Extra!

● Read aloud Ruth 1:16-17. Discuss the meaning of loyalty. Have kids complete the sentence "Loyalty means…" Then ask: **Who is your "Naomi"? Who would you be willing to commit to in the way that Ruth committed to Naomi?** Allow time for kids to respond and then say: **Tell that person this week about your loyalty to him or her.**

● Have kids write stories about Naomi's other daughter-in-law, Orpah, and what might have become of her.

Extra! Extra! Extra! Extra! Extra! Extra!

Giant Removal

As kids hear how David defeated Goliath, they'll discover the excitement of overcoming a big challenge with God's help.

Musical

Supplies: Bibles, paper, and pencils

Preparation: none

Have kids take turns reading aloud 1 Samuel 17:1-58. Then have kids think of nine sounds that might have been heard the day David killed Goliath. For example, kids might suggest laughter, taunting, the clinking of armor, or a terrible thud. Try to keep kids' ideas from becoming too graphic. Write each sound on a slip of paper.

Distribute paper and pencils. Have each child divide his or her papers into nine squares by drawing two vertical lines across the entire length of the paper and two horizontal lines across the entire width of the paper. Read off the sounds, and have kids write each sound in a different square on their papers until their squares are filled. Kids can write any sound in any one of their squares.

After kids have written their sounds, read the sounds aloud again. Each time you read a sound, have kids draw an X through that sound on their papers. Play this game like Bingo, with a Bingo consisting of three sounds in a row in any direction. For added fun, have kids imitate each sound as you read it. Play until you have three Bingos or you run out of sounds.

Close the activity by saying: **There was certainly a lot going on that day! Goliath thought it would be easy to defeat the Israelite army. But with God by his side, David was the one who won the victory.**

Visual

Supplies: One three-foot cardboard square and one five-foot cardboard square, markers or crayons, scissors or a craft knife, scrap cardboard, tape, a chair, and an instant-print camera

Preparation: Before class, prepare the cardboard squares. If you can get a large appliance box, your job will be easy! Simply cut the box apart. If you have to use smaller boxes, you may need to tape the box panels together.

Set out the cardboard and the markers or crayons. Have kids draw a picture of David on the three-foot cardboard square and a picture of Goliath on the five-foot cardboard square. Cut out each figure's face, leaving the bordering hair intact, as shown in the margin.

After you've finished cutting out the faces, use scrap cardboard to make stands for the figures, as shown in the margin.

Say: **Step right up! David, show your bravery by facing Goliath! Goliath, show your most menacing snarl for your little Israelite challenger.**

Have kids take turns standing behind the cardboard figures and placing their faces in the ovals. Kids may have to stand on a stool or chair to play Goliath.

Encourage kids who are standing behind the figures to role play the exchange between David and Goliath. Other kids can pretend to be the armies cheering on their champions.

Take instant-print photos of kids as they stand behind the figures. Give each child a photo to take home. (If you can't get an instant-print camera, use a regular camera. Get the pictures developed before your next class, and mail them to kids as affirmations.)

PHYSICAL

Supplies: Slingshots, table tennis balls, and a paper target

Preparation: Prepare a large target for kids to shoot at. If you're feeling artistic, draw a snarling face on your target to represent Goliath!

Say: **We know David defeated Goliath using stones and a slingshot. Let's see what that might have been like by shooting table tennis ball "stones" at a paper target.**

Set up the target, and have kids practice shooting the balls at it with the slingshots. For fun, move the target around. For example, you might begin with the target set up at kids' eye level and then gradually raise it higher. (Remember, Goliath was about nine feet tall!) Afterward, ask:

● **How easy or hard was it to use the slingshots? Explain.**
● **How easy or hard was it to hit the target? To hit the target's center?**

Say: **It wouldn't have been easy for David to defeat Goliath by himself. He had to aim at a target way over his head, and he probably couldn't get as close to Goliath as you got to our target today. But David knew God would help him. We don't face Goliath every day, but we do face many scary and challenging experiences in life. God can help us overcome our big challenges just as he helped David overcome Goliath.**

VERBAL

Supplies: A Bible, paper, and pencils

Preparation: none

Form groups of four, and give each group Bibles, paper, and pencils. Say: **Often, teachers give you puzzles to work on. But today you're going to do something even more challenging. You're going to create a puzzle for others in our class. Choose whether you'd like to create a crossword puzzle, a word search, or some other kind of puzzle.**

First, read 1 Samuel 17 and choose eight to ten words to use in your puzzle. Then create your puzzle.

Allow at least fifteen minutes for kids to create their puzzles. Then have groups switch puzzles and complete them. Close by saying: **Good job solving each other's puzzles! Those puzzles were a challenge, just as it was a challenge for David to fight Goliath. When you face other challenges this week, remember to look to God for help. Your friends can also help you, just as they helped you solve the puzzles.**

Logical

Supplies: Scratch paper, pencils, a tape measure, and calculators (optional)

Preparation: none

How tall was Goliath? Logical learners will love trying to figure it out! You can do this activity in groups or have kids work alone.

Distribute paper and pencils and challenge kids to estimate how many kids it would take to measure up to Goliath's height. Then have them guess which kids' heights added together would come closest to Goliath's height. Goliath was over nine feet tall. Use a tape measure to determine whose estimate is closest.

Interpersonal

Supplies: A small stuffed animal (optional)

Preparation: none

Say: **King Saul's soldiers were afraid of Goliath. We're all afraid of something. I'll start by telling something I'm afraid of and then we'll go around the circle. Tell something that frightens you. No laughing allowed.**

Go around the circle, or pass around an object such as a small stuffed animal. After everyone has shared, go around again. Have kids each pray for the person on their left. Then thank God for being bigger than any of our "giants."

Reflective

Supplies: A smooth stone for each child and fine-tipped markers

Preparation: none

Set out the markers, and give each child a stone. Say: **The Israelites had to face a scary giant. Goliath made fun of God. He challenged the Israelites' faith. What are you facing? It may be something you're afraid of or an obstacle you have to overcome. It may be someone that's challenging your faith. Ask God to help you discover your "giant." Then write it on your stone. Take your stone home as a reminder that God can help you.**

Allow time for kids to reflect and then close in prayer.

EXTRA! EXTRA! EXTRA! EXTRA! EXTRA!

● Form a Giant-Slayers Prayer Club. Whenever there is a problem in your church, have kids pray together, asking God to knock the giant problem down. Keep track of solved problems that kids have "slain" with their prayers and God's help.

● View the "David and Goliath" song section on the *Donut All Stars* video (available from Integrity) or *Battle of David and Goliath: Truth or Myth?* from the Ancient Secrets of the Bible video series (available from Group Publishing).

● Create a fun play with overhead transparencies by using the "David and Goliath" skit in *Big Action Bible Skits* (available from Group Publishing.)

EXTRA! EXTRA! EXTRA! EXTRA! EXTRA!

Heroine of the Day

As they learn about Esther's courage, kids will discover that God can bring about positive results from their right actions.

 PHYSICAL

Supplies: Bibles

Preparation: None. If you have Bible-character costumes or other props, kids would enjoy using them for this activity.

Form four groups, and give each group a Bible. Assign one of the following characters to each group: Esther, Mordecai, Haman, and King Xerxes. Paraphrase Esther 3:1–8:17, and tell groups to pay close attention to the roles that their specific characters played in the story.

After you have paraphrased the Scripture, say: **Esther has just been declared the queen, and now she has a terrible problem. Your groups are going to act out the problem, beginning with Haman's conversation with King Xerxes about Haman's plot.**

Have the Haman and King Xerxes groups act out this part of the story. Follow along in your Bible to keep the story moving and to prompt groups to act out their parts at the appropriate times. Any child in a group may speak, but only one child may speak at a time.

Continue through the end of the story, asking other groups to join in at the appropriate times. Then say: **Esther wasn't afraid to stand up for her people, even though she could have lost her life. This week when you're tempted to look the other way instead of standing up for what's right, remember Esther's courage.**

VISUAL

Supplies: Ice trays, cups, and small toys such as plastic rings, marbles, bouncy balls, or miniature cars

Preparation: Before class, fill ice trays with water and drop a small toy in each ice-tray section. Freeze until solid. You'll need one "ice-cube surprise" for each child.

When kids arrive, give them each an ice cube in a cup. Don't point out the surprises in the ice cubes. Let kids discover the surprises on their own.

Once kids discover the surprises, challenge them to use whatever means necessary to retrieve the surprises from the ice cubes. For example, kids might sit on the ice cubes or place them under hot water. Tell kids not to put the ice cubes in their mouths.

After kids have retrieved the surprises, ask:

● **How did you feel when you discovered your hidden surprise?**

● **How do you think Esther felt when she discovered that God had a hidden purpose for her?**

Say: **Your life is like the surprise in the ice cube. As you continue to grow in your relationship with God, you'll discover that God has hidden purposes for you.**

Read aloud Jeremiah 31:3 and then thank God for the kindness he continues to show to the kids in your class.

Verbal

Supplies: Bibles, photocopies of the "Modern-Day Esthers" handout, scissors, paper, and pencils

Preparation: Photocopy the "Modern-Day Esthers" handout (p. 62), and cut apart the case studies. You'll need one case study for every four kids.

Form groups of four. Give each group a different case study from the "Modern-Day Esthers" handout, paper, and pencils. Have groups read their case studies and then write stories about the modern-day Esthers in their case studies.

After groups have written their stories, have each group meet with another group and have groups read their stories to each other. When all the stories have been read, say: **We often think that we need to be rich, powerful, or important to make a difference or to fight injustice. But really, all we need to do is stand up for what's right, as Esther did. Just like Esther, you can make a difference in your world.**

Musical

Supplies: none

Preparation: none

Form groups of four. Have each group make up a song about Esther to a familiar tune such as "Jesus Loves Me," "Twinkle, Twinkle, Little Star" "Three Blind Mice" or "Old MacDonald Had a Farm." When groups are finished, have them take turns performing their songs for the class.

Logical

Supplies: Newsprint and a marker or a chalkboard and chalk

Preparation: none

Say: **Although Esther was outwardly beautiful, she was also known for her inner beauty. Let's determine what makes someone beautiful on the outside and on the inside.**

Draw a line down the center of a sheet of newsprint or a chalkboard. On one side of the line, write the word "outer." On the other side of the line, write the word "inner." Have kids call out beauty traits. After each trait is named, have kids determine if that trait represents inner or outer beauty. Then write the trait on the appropriate section of the newsprint or chalkboard.

Afterward, ask:

● **Which collection of beauty traits is valued more in our society? Explain.**

● **Which collection of beauty traits is most pleasing to God? Explain.**

● **Which beauty traits would you most like to have? Explain.**

Say: **Just as Esther was beautiful, each one of you is beautiful in** your own special ways. Although the world sometimes focuses only on outer beauty, God sees what's in our hearts.

InterPersonal

Supplies: One roll of crepe paper streamers for every four kids

Preparation: none

Say: **Our actions affect others; we are connected. Esther realized that her own life was connected to the lives of her people, and that if she didn't intervene, she'd be killed too. Let's play a game now that will remind us that we're all connected.**

Have kids line up single file in teams of four. Give each team a roll of crepe paper streamers. Have the first person in each line wrap the crepe paper twice around one of his or her wrists. Then have the first person pass the crepe paper to the next person, who wraps it twice around one of his or her wrists in the same manner. Have kids continue wrapping the crepe paper around their wrists until everyone is connected. If a team's crepe paper breaks, the team must start again.

After the kids in each team are connected to each other, have the teams walk around the room. Then have teams remove their crepe paper and ask:

● **What was hard about getting connected? What was easy?**

● **What actions did you take during this game that affected others on your team?**

● **What actions do you take at school that affect others? at home? at church?**

Say: **Our actions can affect others in positive and negative ways. Esther's actions affected herself and her people in a positive way. So think before you act, and try to choose actions with positive effects.**

Reflective

Supplies: A Bible

Preparation: none

Say: **Haman was prejudiced. He hated the Jewish people even though he didn't know very many of them. He hated them simply because of who they were. Sometimes we hate people, too. We are prejudiced toward people because of the way they look, or where they're from, or how they dress.**

I'm going to read a Bible passage. After I read it, let's be silent for a while and ask God to show us any prejudice we have in our hearts. Then we can confess our sins of prejudice to God.

Read aloud Psalm 139:23-24. After three minutes of silence, pray: **God, we confess to you our prejudices. Please forgive us and cleanse us of our sins. Amen.**

EXTRA! EXTRA! EXTRA! EXTRA! EXTRA!

- Make Queen Esther awards using various craft supplies. Give these awards to people who have demonstrated courage in helping others.

- Have kids imagine that they're planning Esther's banquet. Help them create a menu of foods that people may have eaten in Esther's day. Consult reference books if necessary. If you have cooking facilities available, plan a time to prepare your banquet.

- Create a fun play with overhead transparencies by using the "Esther" skit in *Big Action Bible Skits* (available from Group Publishing.)

EXTRA! EXTRA! EXTRA! EXTRA! EXTRA!

MoDERN-DAY ESTHERS

case STUDY 1

At school, Sheila learns that everyone is picking on the kids in the special education class. What can she do?

case STUDY 2

Nicholas learns that a factory is dumping toxic waste into a local river. What can he do?

---

case STUDY 3

Ryan discovers that his city's government is tearing down the only houses in town that poor people can afford. What can he do?

case STUDY 4

Shania learns that her church's governing board is cutting all funding for children's programs. What can she do?

 # What's for Lunch?

As they hear
how Daniel faced
the lions rather
than not
praying, kids will
be encouraged to
stand up for
their faith.

Visual

Supplies: Enlarged photocopies of "Story Masks" faces, scissors, markers or crayons, poster board, glue, aluminum foil, and craft sticks

Preparation: Use a photocopier to enlarge the faces on the "Story Masks" hand-out (pp. 67-68). Each face will need to be large enough to cover a child's face. You'll need one Daniel, one King Darius, and enough lions and spectators so that each child can have a mask. If you want the masks to be more elaborate, you could also provide yarn and felt scraps to be used to make hair and facial features.

Ask:

● **How many of you have ever worn costumes or masks? Tell me about it.**

Allow kids to respond and then say: **We wear masks or costumes when we want to pretend to be someone we're not. Our Bible story today is about a man named Daniel who was asked to be someone he was not. Daniel was a good man who prayed and worshiped God. The king wanted Daniel to quit praying to God. We're going to make story masks to help tell Daniel's story.**

Distribute the faces you've prepared. Assign one child to be Daniel, one to be King Darius, two to be soldiers, and the rest to be lions and spectators. Have kids cut out and color the faces and then glue the faces to poster board. Then have kids trim the poster board to match their face outlines. Have the kids who are playing the soldiers sculpt aluminum foil helmets on the tops of their masks.

Mount the finished story masks on craft sticks. Then practice using the masks to tell Daniel's story as described in the Physical activity below.

Physical

Supplies: A Bible and story masks from the Visual activity

Preparation: If you didn't do the Visual activity, prepare enlarged photocopies of the "Story Masks" (pp. 67-68) for children to use. Make arrangements with the teacher of a younger class for your kids to present the story of Daniel to his or her class.

Distribute the story masks kids made during the Visual activity. Read Daniel 6:1-28 aloud, and have children act out their parts while you read. You may need to repeat the story a few times before children are completely comfortable with their actions.

After you've practiced, have your kids use the masks to act out the story for a younger class. Take time afterward for the younger kids to talk to the characters. Encourage them to ask questions such as "Daniel, were you scared of all those lions?" "King Darius, why didn't you let Daniel pray?" or "Lions, why didn't you eat Daniel up?" Encourage kids to answer the questions in character.

Leave the masks with the younger children for their storytelling fun.

VERBAL

Supplies: Bibles; unlined paper; card stock; thick, dark-colored markers; pencils; and tape or pins

Preparation: none

Form groups of two to four, and distribute Bibles; scratch paper; unlined paper; card stock; pencils; and thick, dark-colored markers. Have one person in each group read aloud Daniel 6:1-28. Then have each group think of ten words that describe Daniel.

Have each group use a marker to draw a large outline of a lion on card stock. Then have groups cover their lion outlines with blank sheets of unlined paper. Have kids write the words that describe Daniel along the outlines to create lion-shaped "Wuzzles," as shown in the margin.

Have group members write their names on their group's Wuzzle. Then display all the Wuzzles on a wall or bulletin board. Invite kids in each group to read their words aloud.

Close the activity by saying: **Daniel was an amazing man. He could have been eaten by those lions, but he wasn't afraid. He knew God would protect him. God will protect us, too.**

MUSICAL

Supplies: Paper, a marker, tape, a small box or hat, a music CD or cassette, and a CD or cassette player

Preparation: Tape three pieces of paper with the numbers 1, 2, and 3 written on them to three doors or walls in your room. Put slips of paper numbered 1, 2, and 3 into a small box or hat.

Play music as the children walk from one numbered door or wall to the next. When you stop the music, children must stand next to the door or wall they're closest to.

After children have gathered by the doors, draw a number from the hat or box you've prepared. Announce that the number you've drawn is now the lions' den. Inform the kids standing next to that door or wall that they've just been gobbled up. Have those kids sit in the middle of the floor.

Continue playing until there are only three children left. At this point, tell the remaining participants that each one of them must go to a different door. Play until there is only one child left.

Then ask:
● **How did it feel to wait to be eaten by the lions?**
● **How is this like or unlike the way Daniel may've felt?**
● **Why did Daniel trust God?**
● **What is something you're facing that you really need to trust God about?**
Close by praying for children and the things they mentioned.

LOGICAL

Supplies: A Bible, pencils, and paper

Preparation: None. If you have graph paper available, kids might enjoy using it for this activity.

Ask:

● **When have you felt tension at home? with your friends? at school?**

Say: **Daniel must have felt a lot of tension when he heard about the king's decree. He knew he wasn't supposed to pray, but he knew he had to keep praying. Let's monitor the tension level in Daniel's life as we read his story.**

Distribute paper and pencils, and have kids chart the tension in the Bible story. As you read aloud Daniel 6:1-28, have each child draw a continuous line on his or her paper that represents the level of tension in the story. For example, kids may begin by drawing straight horizontal lines. As you read verse 4, when the king's other advisors begin accusing Daniel, kids' lines may rise sharply.

After you finish reading, have kids show and explain their tension graphs to the rest of the class.

Ask:

● **What would your tension graph have looked like if you had been Daniel?**

● **When is it hardest to do what's right?**

● **What helps you to do the right thing even when it's hard?**

Say: **Daniel obeyed God even when it was hard. We can learn a lot about faith and obedience from Daniel's life.**

INTERPERSONAL

Supplies: none

Preparation: none

Lead kids in a Lions' Den Challenge. Form pairs. Have partners take turns proposing situations that might make the other partner deny his or her faith. After each situation is proposed, have the other partner tell how he or she would obey God.

For example, a child might propose, "Your principal says you can't go out for recess unless you say you don't believe in Jesus." His or her partner might respond, "So I skip recess all year." Or someone might suggest, "Your friends laugh at you because you go to church." His or her partner might respond, "I keep going anyway and make new friends at church."

Encourage kids to help each other stand up for their faith at school this week!

REFLECTIVE

Supplies: none

Preparation: none

Say: **Think silently about someone you know who's like Daniel. Who can you think of who has stood up for his or her faith in a difficult circumstance? What has that person done to demonstrate his or** her commitment to his or her faith?

Allow a few moments for kids to reflect and then say: **There are modern-day Daniels all around us. They're not perfect people, but they do have courageous faith. Use the person you thought of as a role model to help you be courageous in your faith this week.**

EXTRA! EXTRA! EXTRA! EXTRA! EXTRA!

- Play Lions' Den Tag with three lions and one Daniel. Once a lion tags a person, that person is frozen. Daniel is the only one who can "unfreeze" frozen people. Daniel can't be frozen because he's full of faith.

- Daniel had prayer dates with God three times a day. Have kids make prayer dates with God. Have them write on sheets of paper the time, the place, and what they'll take on their dates with God.

- Create a fun play with overhead transparencies by using the "Daniel in the Lions' Den" skit in *Big Action Bible Skits* (available from Group Publishing.)

EXTRA! EXTRA! EXTRA! EXTRA! EXTRA!

STORY MASKS

DANIEL

KING DARIUS

Forget-Me-Not Bible Story Activities

67

STORY MASKS

LION

BIBLE-TIMES PERSON

Swallowed Up

Kids will discover the importance of obedience as they explore Jonah's story in fun new ways.

Visual

Supplies: A Bible and two or three skeins of yarn

Preparation: Select a location outdoors or in a gymnasium or fellowship hall where kids can create a giant fish.

Paraphrase the story of Jonah from Jonah 1:1–3:10. Ask:

● **How big do you think this big fish was? Bigger than your house? Bigger than our church building? Bigger than your school?**

Say: **The Bible doesn't say how big the fish was. But we know it was big enough to swallow Jonah whole after he was thrown overboard. Let's go outside and demonstrate how big this fish might have been.**

Go to your designated location, and give kids two or three skeins of yarn. Have kids work together to hold the yarn and create the shape of the fish. You'll need to designate a "fishtail" person to stand still and hold the end of the yarn while everyone else moves into position.

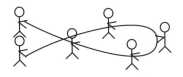

When kids finish their fish shape, encourage them to have a little fun with it by wiggling the fish's fins, "swimming" across the lawn (or room), or opening the fish's mouth to spit Jonah out.

Verbal

Supplies: none

Preparation: none

Have kids sit in a circle on the floor. Say: **This is a story circle. We're going to imagine what it was like to be inside the big fish. We'll go around the circle. On your turn, add a description of the inside of the fish. You can't repeat anyone else's description. I'll start. It was dark inside the big fish.**

If kids are stumped, ask questions to get their imaginations going, such as "What do you think Jonah smelled like?" or "What else do you think was inside that fish's belly?"

Continue until everyone has had a turn. If you have six or fewer kids, go around the circle again.

After your story circle is finished, ask:

● **How do you think Jonah felt when he was inside the big fish?**

● **How do you feel when you're in a dark, scary place in your life?**

● **Do you think God was with Jonah inside the fish, even though Jonah had disobeyed God?**

● **Do you think God is with you, even when you've disobeyed him and you're feeling scared and alone?**

Say: **God is always with us, even when we've disobeyed him and tried to run away from what he wants us to do. God wants us to** obey him, and he doesn't want us to feel scared and alone like we sometimes do when we disobey.

♫ MUSICAL

Supplies: none

Preparation: Practice singing "Jonah, Jonah" so you can teach it to your class.

Teach children "Jonah, Jonah" to the tune of "Old MacDonald Had a Farm." Encourage kids to display thumbs-up and thumbs-down signs when they sing the words "Thumbs up? Thumbs down! No way!" or "Thumbs up? Thumbs down! Hooray!" Invite kids to help you make up motions to go with the rest of the words.

JONAH, JONAH

Jonah, Jonah ran away.
Thumbs up? Thumbs down! No way!
He ran from God and disobeyed.
Thumbs up? Thumbs down! No way!
He jumped a ship, took a trip;
Jonah, Jonah, that's not hip!
Jonah, Jonah ran away.
Thumbs up? Thumbs down! No way!

Jonah, Jonah overboard—
Shoulda listened to the Lord!
Wrapped up in a seaweed cord…
Shoulda listened to the Lord!
Big fish swam up, gulped him down.
Slimy seaweed all around!
Jonah, Jonah overboard—
Shoulda listened to the Lord!

Jonah, Jonah knelt to pray.
Thumbs down? Thumbs up! Hooray!
"God, help me out—I will obey."
Thumbs down? Thumbs up! Hooray!
With a burp, slurp, whee and a flee, fly, soar,
Jonah landed on the shore.
Jonah, Jonah knelt to pray.
Thumbs down? Thumbs up! Hooray!

After you sing the song, say: **Jonah did some pretty stupid things. Instead of obeying God, he ran away in the opposite direction. But of course God could see him. Sometimes we ignore God's directions, just as Jonah did. Next time you're tempted to ignore God's directions and do things your own way, remember Jonah and listen to the Lord!**

Logical

Supplies: Two or three skeins of yarn and masking tape

Preparation: Arrange for several adult classes (or better yet, your entire congregation!) to meet you outdoors or in a gymnasium or fellowship hall.

Have kids use the yarn to make the fish shape as described in the Visual activity. Then have children sit in their spots, keeping the fish shape intact. Work with kids until they agree on an exact number for each of the following questions. Ask:

● **How many buildings the size of our church building could fit inside this big fish?**

● **How many fish this size would fill our church building?**

● **How many of our church members would fill this fish?**

After kids have agreed on their answers, bring out your group of adults and have them crowd side by side into the fish shape. If there's still room in the fish shape after everyone has crowded in, use masking tape to mark off where the people end and then have people move over the tape line to fill out the rest of the fish.

Put kids in charge of counting the people. Afterward, compare their estimate and the actual number. Say: **If this many people could fit inside our big fish, just imagine how many little fish could fit inside! I bet that fish's belly was slimy and stinky and disgusting because of all the little fish it had eaten. I'm sure being in that yucky place taught Jonah a good lesson about obeying God.**

Physical

Supplies: none

Preparation: none

Say: **We're going to play a game of Fish Bait. Because Jonah chose not to obey God, he became fish bait for a very large fish.**

Choose two kids to be a big fish. Explain that the two children must stay together as though they're one big fish. They must never lose contact with one another. Have the big fish chase the other children. When someone is tagged, that person becomes part of the big fish. Play until everyone is caught.

After the game, say: **Eventually the big fish caught up with all of us. Like Jonah, we may think we can run and hide when we disobey God, but eventually our disobedience will catch up with us and get us into trouble. Remember to obey God this week.**

Interpersonal

Supplies: One die for every two children in your class

Preparation: none

Form pairs. Give each pair a die. Have partners roll their dice. Whatever number a pair rolls, each partner in the pair has to think of that many ways they've seen the other partner obey God. For example, kids may say, "You come to church" or "You don't lie."

If you don't want to use numbered dice, use alphabet cubes from a word game such as Boggle. Have each partner use the letters he or she rolls to suggest ways they've seen the other partner obey God. For example, A could mean "Always comes to church" or "Asks parents' permission to do things."

After kids have finished, say: **I heard a lot of good ideas about obeying God. Keep up your obedience this week!**

# REFlective

Supplies: Paper and markers

Preparation: none

Give each child a sheet of paper and a marker. Have each child draw a large fish shape on his or her paper. Then have kids think about their answers to the following questions to help them reflect on where they would have fit into Jonah's story. Ask:

● **Would you have been the sinful Ninevites who needed God's forgiveness?**

● **Would you have been the sailors on the boat who unknowingly helped someone disobey God?**

● **Would you have been Jonah when he out and out disobeyed God?**

● **Would you have been Jonah when he finally listened to God and did what was right?**

Say: **Think about who you would have been in the story if you had been there, and write the name of that person or people on your fish. Then talk to God about where you are in your relationship with him. You may need to ask God for forgiveness or for strength. Ask God to help you become like Jonah when he obeyed.**

Allow time for kids to reflect and pray and then close in prayer.

EXTRA! EXTRA! EXTRA! EXTRA! EXTRA!

● Simulate the sensations and smells Jonah might have experienced when he was inside the fish. Put boiled eggs, cooked spaghetti, and sardines in a bowl. Cover the bowl with a dark-colored trash bag. Have kids put their hands into the bag and feel the "fish guts."

● Play a variation on the game Red Rover. Instead of saying "Red Rover, Red Rover, let (name) come over," have kids say "To Nineveh, to Nineveh, let (name) come in-eveh!" Play this game with the same rules as regular Red Rover.

● Create a fun play with overhead transparencies by using the "Jonah and the Big Fish" skit in *Big Action Bible Skits* (available from Group Publishing.)

EXTRA! EXTRA! EXTRA! EXTRA! EXTRA!

Preparing the Way

Kids will consider what they can do to "prepare the way" for Jesus as they hear how John prepared people for Jesus' coming.

Visual

Supplies: Bibles, fine-tipped permanent markers, overhead transparency sheets, a paper cutter, slide mounts, a slide projector, and a projection screen

Preparation: Purchase slide mounts from a photofinishing store. You'll need at least twelve slide mounts. Use a paper cutter to cut the overhead transparency sheets into small squares to fit into the slide mounts. Set up a slide projector and a projection screen to show the finished slides. (If you don't have a slide projector, have kids draw their pictures on whole transparency sheets, and display them on an overhead projector.)

Form six groups. Distribute Bibles, and assign each group one of the following Scripture passages: Matthew 3:1-3; Matthew 3:4; Matthew 3:5-6; Matthew 3:7-8; Matthew 3:11-12; and Matthew 3:13-15.

Give each group fine-tipped permanent markers and two or more transparency squares and slide mounts. Have groups draw pictures of their Scripture passages on the transparency squares. Help kids put their finished pictures into the slide mounts.

Put the finished slides into a slide projector in sequence and then have a "John the Baptist" slide show on the projection screen. Have groups read their Scripture passages and then tell about their slides. If you want, invite another class to join you for the show!

Verbal

Supplies: A Bible, pencils, index cards, and a basic cookbook (optional)

Preparation: none

Form pairs. Read Matthew 3:1-6 aloud. Say: **John was an unusual character. He wandered around in the desert wearing camel's-hair clothing, and he ate locusts and wild honey. Just for fun, we're going to see how many recipes for locusts and wild honey we can dream up. For example, you might create a recipe for chopped locust-chip cookies or locust-crunch breakfast cereal. Work with your partner to create a recipe, complete with ingredients and preparation instructions.**

Distribute pencils and index cards. If you have a basic cookbook, set it out so kids can refer to it for recipe ideas and ingredients. Have pairs write their finished recipes on the cards.

After kids have finished writing their recipes, have pairs share their creations with the class. Then say: **We don't know what locusts and honey tasted like, but we do know honey is sweet. In Psalm 119:103 the Bible says that God's promises are even sweeter than honey. It was John's job to announce that God had kept his promise to send a Savior, Jesus Christ.**

 MUSICAL

Supplies: Various craft supplies, empty containers of various sizes, paper plates, rocks, sand, glue, tape, a stapler, and sandpaper

Preparation: Gather empty containers such as tubs for yogurt, cottage cheese, or margarine.

Say: **John the Baptist spent a lot of time in the desert. We're going to make music with something he probably saw a lot of—sand.**

Set out the rocks, sand, sandpaper, and other supplies. Encourage kids to experiment with the different materials and create as many different-sounding instruments as they can. For example, they might glue sandpaper to large rocks to create cymbals or fill containers with sand to create maracas.

When kids have finished their instruments, have them use their instruments to play "God Is So Good" or another familiar praise song.

 LOGICAL

Supplies: Bibles, pencils, paper, newsprint, and a marker

Preparation: None. If you know someone in your church who's a good artist, invite him or her to sketch kids' modern-day John the Baptist in a contemporary environment. If not, have fun creating the sketch yourself—the sillier, the better.

Form five groups. Tell kids that they're going to imagine that John the Baptist is alive today. Say: **If John the Baptist were alive today, what would his lifestyle be like? What kind of house would he live in—or would he live in a house at all? How would he get around? Would he still be roaming the desert? Would he ride a bike or take a bus? What would a modern-day John the Baptist be like?**

Distribute Bibles, paper, and pencils, and assign each group one of the following categories: home, transportation, clothing, pets, and occupation.

Allow about five minutes for kids to make notes about their assigned categories. Then call groups back together. Have kids read their category descriptions. As they read, draw a simple sketch of John the Baptist in his modern environment.

After all the groups have shared, step back and look at the finished sketch. Say: **Our modern-day John the Baptist looks a lot different than the one described in the Bible. But I'm sure if John the Baptist were alive today, his goal in life would be the same: to tell people about Jesus. We can tell people about Jesus too.**

 PHYSICAL

Supplies: Modern-day John the Baptist category descriptions from the Logical activity or newsprint and a marker and a camcorder (optional)

Preparation: If you didn't do the Logical activity, have kids quickly brainstorm a description of a modern-day John the Baptist. Record kids' ideas on a sheet of newsprint or a chalkboard.

Form five groups, or have kids stay in their groups from the Logical activity. Choose a volunteer who can really ham it up to act as the host of your class show: "Lifestyles of the Poor and Famous." Have the host go from group to group and interview the kids about John's lifestyle. Encourage kids to refer to their group's category description (or the newsprint list if you didn't complete the Logical activity) for ideas.

For example, the host may say in his or her best British accent: "I understand you know something about the man named John the Baptist. What can you tell me to help me—and all our viewers of the 'Lifestyles of the Poor and Famous'—know him better?"

Encourage kids to use actions in their descriptions of John's lifestyle. For example, if they suggest that he lives in a rickety shack, kids might join hands and lean from side to side. If kids suggest that John has a pet tarantula, they might crawl all around the host. Let kids' imaginations take over!

If you want, videotape your show and schedule a time you can all watch it together.

 InterPersonal

Supplies: none

Preparation: none

Form pairs. Say: **John the Baptist gave up many things in his passion to prepare the way for the Lord. He didn't have a nice house, nice clothes, or even much to eat. Share with your partner the things you've given up to tell others about Jesus—or the things you'd be willing to give up.**

After partners have had time to share, ask:
● **Which things would be most difficult for you to give up? Why?**

Close by having partners pray together about the things they've discussed.

ReFlective

Supplies: none

Preparation: none

Ask kids to think silently about their answers to these questions:
● **What have you done to prepare the way for the Lord at home?**
● **What have you done to prepare the way for the Lord in your neighborhood?**
● **What have you done to prepare the way for the Lord at school?**

Allow a few minutes for kids to reflect and then close by praying: **Lord, please help us prepare the way for you wherever we go, whatever we do, and with whoever we meet this week. Amen.**

EXTRA! EXTRA! EXTRA! EXTRA! EXTRA!

● Make this Sandy Sundae snack for each child. Pour finely ground graham crackers into one-fourth of a clear cup. Stir in five raisins. Then pour vanilla pudding over the graham cracker layer until the cup is half full. Add another layer of graham crackers and raisins and then another layer of pudding. Serve the snack and remind kids that John the Baptist ate locusts and honey in the desert.

● Form pairs. Point out that John the Baptist was bold in his preaching about Jesus. Then have partners discuss what it means to be bold in our faith today. Have each child come up with the boldest thing he or she could possibly do to share his or her faith. Encourage kids to do their bold things this week.

EXTRA! EXTRA! EXTRA! EXTRA! EXTRA!

Anything's Possible

Kids will discover God's power as they hear about Jesus walking on water.

Visual

Supplies: A Bible, various colors of liquid tempera paint, water, an ice tray, a spoon, newspapers, and white paper

Preparation: Place a few drops of liquid tempera paint into each ice-tray section. Carefully add water to fill the tray and then stir the contents of each section. Freeze. Bring the frozen paint-cubes to class and keep them frozen. Leave them in your church kitchen's freezer, if necessary, until you're ready to use them.

Read aloud Mark 6:45-56. Cover a work area with newspapers and then set out the frozen paint-cubes and blank sheets of white paper. Have kids use the paint cubes and paper to illustrate the story. When kids finish their pictures, have them show each other what they've created.

Then ask:

● **How did Jesus walk on water?**

● **How could someone walk on water today?**

● **What does this Bible story teach you about what Jesus can do?**

Say: **The only way we can walk on water today is if the water is frozen like these ice cubes. The water Jesus walked on wasn't frozen. Jesus is God, and he has the power to do anything imaginable. Take your pictures home to remind you of this story that shows us how powerful our God is.**

Verbal

Supplies: Newsprint and a marker or a chalkboard and chalk

Preparation: none

Have kids think of "God sightings"—times they've seen God do miraculous things in their lives or in the lives of others they know. Kids can also include miracles they've heard about in the news. If kids are stumped, remind them that miracles don't have to be outwardly spectacular. Point out that sometimes miracles take place in people's hearts or attitudes.

List these modern-day miracles on newsprint or a chalkboard. After you finish your list, say: **We may think miracles have to be spectacular, like walking on water. But miracles can happen to anyone at any time. It's great that God still makes miracles happen in our lives.**

Pray, thanking God for his miraculous power.

Musical

Supplies: A cassette recorder, a blank cassette tape, buckets, spray bottles, empty soda bottles with lids, sieves, funnels, and lots of water

Preparation: If possible, arrange to have this lesson in a room with a water faucet. If the weather's nice, it would be fun to do this activity outdoors.

Say: **Have you ever stopped to listen to the sounds of water? If you listen closely, you'll hear an entire orchestra of sounds. We're going to make music with water so we can hear some of the sounds Jesus' disciples may have heard on their many trips out to sea.**

Set out the supplies you've brought. Have kids work together to create water sounds. Then have them synchronize their water sounds into a harmony. Tape-record five minutes of kids' water music. (If you do this activity before the Visual activity, you can play the recording as kids create their story pictures.)

Play back the recording, then say: **It's amazing to hear all the different sounds we've made with water. In addition to these sounds, the disciples heard the sounds of waves crashing against their boat. The wind was blowing so hard that the disciples were having a hard time rowing. But Jesus instantly calmed the wind and waves. He can calm our stormy lives, too.**

Logical

Supplies: Bibles and newsprint and a marker or a chalkboard and chalk (optional)

Preparation: Read the Scriptures kids will be studying in this activity.

Form groups of four. Say: **In addition to walking on water, Jesus did many other amazing miracles. We're going to compare and contrast the miracle we've been learning about today with other miracles described in the Bible.**

Distribute Bibles, and have kids read these Scriptures: Mark 6:45-56; John 2:1-11; and Mark 6:30-44. Have kids compare and contrast the three miracles by answering the following questions. You may want to write the questions on a sheet of newsprint or a chalkboard so kids can refer to them during their discussions.
- What's different about these miracles? similar?
- Which miracle impresses you the most? Explain.
- What does each miracle reveal about Jesus?

After about ten minutes, invite kids to share their responses. Then say: **Jesus' miracles demonstrate his love and compassion as well as his power. Jesus never made miracles happen just to impress people. He used God's power to meet people's needs, and he gave God the glory for the amazing results.**

Physical

Supplies: Bibles

Preparation: Take inventory of your room and consider what supplies kids might use to recreate the Bible story. Bring in additional supplies if you want, but avoid obvious props such as Bible-character costumes (unless you normally keep costumes in your room).

When kids arrive, have them read Mark 6:45-56. Tell them there will be a "test" later. After all the kids have read the Scripture, say: **You're going to recreate the Bible story you just read using only the things in this room. You'll have to be creative.**

Form four groups. Assign one of the following tasks to each group: finding props, creating sound effects, directing actions, and choosing actors.

Allow about ten minutes of preparation time and then have kids present their story.

INTERPERSONAL

Supplies: Pencils, paper, newsprint, and a marker

Preparation: none

Form pairs, and give each pair paper and pencils. Have partners create "Coming Attractions" lists by listing the things they learned from this Bible story. Tell them you'll save their lists to share with the next class who learns about this story.

After pairs have completed their lists, invite them to share their responses. Compile all the responses on a sheet of newsprint.

Use the compiled list in next year's class as an introduction to the story. You may also want to refer to the list at the beginning of your next meeting by having kids share ways they've been able to apply the things they've learned.

REFLECTIVE

Supplies: A Bible

Preparation: none

Read aloud Matthew 14:22-33. Say: **Peter had faith to step out on the water, but he took his eyes off Jesus. When he did, he started sinking. Think silently about one area in your life where you need to trust Jesus and keep your eyes on him. Maybe you're facing a temptation, or maybe there's an area in your life in which you need to have more faith in God.** (Pause two minutes.) **Think about what you'll have to do to keep your eyes on Jesus.**

Close by asking God to help kids keep their focus on Jesus this week.

EXTRA! EXTRA! EXTRA! EXTRA! EXTRA!

● Have kids think of someone who's facing an "impossible" situation. Have kids commit to pray for or with that person so he or she will be able to stay focused on God.

● Have kids create a dance to the water music in the Musical activity.

● Have kids perform their impromptu drama from the Physical activity for another class.

EXTRA! EXTRA! EXTRA! EXTRA! EXTRA!

 Savior Is
Born

Kids will spread

the light of Jesus'

love to each

other as they

celebrate his

birth.

 **VERBAL**

Supplies: Bibles, newsprint and a marker or a chalkboard and chalk, paper, and pencils

Preparation: Write the following questions on newsprint or a chalkboard:

- If Jesus was born today in our city, where would he be born?
- What would his family travel in or on?
- Who would his mother be? What would she be like?
- Who would his father be? What would he be like?
- Who would be the first visitors at Jesus' birth?
- What gifts would they bring?
- Who would the angel appear to, and where would the angel appear?
- What kind of law would our government make today to try to get rid of Jesus?

Form groups of four, and give each group a Bible, pencils, and paper. Say: **We've all heard the story of Jesus' birth—an angel appeared to Mary, Mary and Joseph traveled to Bethlehem, and Jesus was laid in a manger. Today we're going to take those familiar details of Jesus' birth story and modernize them. We're going to imagine what the story of Jesus' birth would've been like if Jesus had been born in our time.**

Read aloud the story of Jesus' birth from Luke 2:1-20. Then work in your groups to answer the questions on the newsprint and write your modern stories of Jesus' birth.

Circulate between the groups to offer help as needed. Encourage kids to use the questions on the newsprint to match their modern details to the biblical details as closely as possible. For example, the gifts the wise men brought were considered extremely valuable in Jesus' time; encourage kids to imagine what gifts would be considered extremely valuable today.

When kids finish their stories, have groups take turns reading them. After all the stories have been read, say: **It's interesting to think of what Jesus' birth might have been like if he'd been born today. Maybe newspapers would announce his birth; maybe presidents would come to visit. One thing is certain: Jesus' birth changed our world forever.**

PHYSICAL

Supplies: Newsprint and a marker or a chalkboard and chalk, small candles that are easy for kids to hold, aluminum foil, and matches

Preparation: List the following on a sheet of newsprint or a chalkboard: baby Jesus, Mary, Joseph, shepherd, wise man, roof, star, angel, manger, gift, and swaddling clothes. If you have more than eleven kids, add to your list various animals or more shepherds, wise men, or angels. Also, use squares of foil to make handles—flared at the top to catch wax—for each of the candles.

Say: **We're going to experience a little bit of Christmas today by creating a living Nativity scene. One at a time, we'll place people in our Nativity scene to represent the Nativity elements I've written on the newsprint. Each time you place someone in our Nativity scene, tell why you chose that person to represent that particular Nativity element. I'll start by choosing someone to represent baby Jesus.**

Turn down the lights. Choose one person to be baby Jesus, and tell why you've chosen him or her. For example, you might say "(Name of child), your love for people reminds me of Jesus." Give that person a lighted candle, and place him or her in the living Nativity scene.

Have baby Jesus choose someone to represent another element of the Nativity. Then have baby Jesus explain his or her choice, place that person in the Nativity, and light that person's candle from his or her own candle.

After everyone has been placed in the Nativity scene and given a candle, read aloud the following Scriptures. As you read, emphasize the underlined words. Don't read the verse references.

"'Arise, shine, for your <u>light has come,</u> and the glory of the Lord rises upon you' " (Isaiah 60:1, NIV).

<u>"I am the light of the world.</u> Whoever follows me will never walk in darkness, but will have the light of life" (John 8:12b, NIV).

"'<u>You are the light of the world.</u>..Let your light shine before men, that they may see your good deeds and praise your Father in heaven' " (Matthew 5:14a, 16b, NIV).

Pause, then continue:

And God said, <u>"Let there be light,"</u> and there was light (Genesis 1:3, NIV).

Pray: **Dear God, thank you for sending Jesus, the light, into a dark world. Help us to be your light and help to reveal Jesus during this Christmas season. Amen.**

Tell kids to blow out their candles, and collect kids' candles before dismissing them or moving on to your next activity.

Visual

Supplies: Several boxes of vanilla wafer cookies, frosting, blunt knives, and Nativity scene figures

Preparation: none

Have kids work together to create an edible Nativity scene. Kids can cut up the wafer cookies and use the frosting as glue to create the stable.

Once the stable is built, have kids tell the story of Jesus' birth as they place the figures in and around the stable. Then enjoy eating the stable.

Musical

Supplies: A CD or cassette of Christmas music and a CD or cassette player (optional)

Preparation: None. If you want, arrange for kids to perform their song for another class.

Have kids do this activity in several small groups or as one large group. Say: **Singing Christmas carols is a fun way to celebrate Jesus' birth. Today we're going to make our Christmas carols even more fun by creating hand motions for them.**

Invite kids to choose a Christmas carol to sing, such as "Silent Night" or "Away in a Manger." Then have kids work together to create hand motions for their chosen song. If you'd like, let kids sing along with a CD or cassette of Christmas music.

When kids have finished creating their hand motions, have them demonstrate their motions. Then have everyone join in as you sing the song with the hand motions.

Logical

Supplies: Bibles, paper, and pencils

Preparation: none

Form groups of three. Distribute Bibles, and have kids read Matthew 2:1-23. Then ask:

● **What would the world be like today if Herod had succeeded in killing Jesus?**

Have kids imagine a world without the good of Christ's influence. If kids need help getting started, prompt kids to consider areas such as crime, entertainment, relationships, politics, and education. Or assign one or two of these areas to each group.

Have each group appoint a recorder to record the group's ideas. After about ten minutes, call groups back together and invite kids to report on their discussions.

After the reports, say: **If Jesus had never grown up, no one would have heard his teaching about God's love. Jesus wouldn't have died on the cross, and it would be impossible for us to be forgiven for our sins. Without God's love and forgiveness, people would be mean and yucky all the time—our world would be a terrible place to live. Let's take a moment to thank God for sending Jesus.**

Have kids return to their groups and spend a few moments praying together. Close by thanking God for the gift of his Son.

Interpersonal

Supplies: Paper, a pencil, a hat or bowl, index cards, red and green fine-tipped markers, glitter and other craft supplies (optional), a hole punch, red ribbon or yarn, scissors, a CD or cassette of Christmas music, and a CD or cassette player

Preparation: Write each child's name on a separate slip of paper. Place the names in a hat or bowl.

Have children draw names from the hat. Make sure each child has someone else's name. Then give each child an index card and a red or green fine-tipped marker. Have kids write the following sentence on their cards: "You are God's gift to me because..." Have kids complete the sentence for the person whose name they drew. For example, kids may write "You are God's gift to me because you make me feel better when I'm sad" or "You are God's gift to me because you've been my friend for six years." Encourage kids to decorate their cards with the markers (and other craft supplies, if you've provided them).

As kids are decorating their cards, go around and punch a hole in one corner of each child's card. Have each child thread two feet of red ribbon or yarn through the hole and knot the ends of the ribbon or yarn together.

After kids finish their gift cards, say: **Now it's time to celebrate the special gift of friends this Christmas.**

Play Christmas music in the background as kids deliver their gift tags to each other.

❖?❖ Reflective

Supplies: Index cards, pencils, and envelopes

Preparation: none

Give each child an index card, an envelope, and a pencil. Ask: **Why does Jesus' birth matter to you? Write an answer on your card. Then put the card in your envelope and seal the envelope.**

Allow a few minutes for kids to write their answers and seal their cards in their envelopes. Once the envelopes are sealed, say: **Do not open your envelope until Christmas next year. Be sure to put your envelope in a place where you'll remember to open it and read it next year. For example, you may want to put it in your Christmas stocking before it's packed away. When you open your envelope next year, you'll be reminded how much Jesus matters in your life.**

Extra! Extra! Extra! Extra! Extra!

● Have kids prepare two or three Christmas carols. Then take them to a nursing home to sing their songs. Have kids dress in Nativity scene costumes for even more fun.

● Give the gift of after-holiday cleaning. While kids are out of school for Christmas break, have them serve church staff members who've been extremely busy during the holidays by cleaning their houses!

● Read *Do You See the Star?*, a fun foldover book from Group Publishing.

EXTRA! EXTRA! EXTRA! EXTRA! EXTRA!

Clean Again

As they hear
how Jesus
healed ten
men with
leprosy, kids will
learn that God
wants us to be
thankful for all
the good things
he gives us.

Interpersonal

Supplies: A Bible and large jingle bells

Preparation: none

Give large jingle bells to one-third of your group. Say: **If you have a bell, you are a leper. Lepers have a terrible disease called leprosy that rots away their skin. In Bible times, lepers had to cry out "Unclean!" whenever they entered a town. Everyone would run from the lepers. During this game, our lepers will ring their bells and move among our group. Lepers, as you ring your bells, say "Unclean!" Anyone you touch catches your leprosy and must fall down as if they're dead.**

After five minutes of this game, stop and collect the bells. Ask:

● **How did those of you with leprosy feel during this game?**

● **How did the rest of you feel?**

● **What would it be like to be a real leper?**

Say: **Today's Bible story is about Jesus reaching into the lives of ten lepers and healing them. Listen as I read Luke 17:11-19.**

Read aloud the Scripture. Then ask:

● **What can we learn about Jesus from this Scripture?**

● **When have you responded to God as the thankful leper did? the unthankful nine?**

● **How would you feel if Jesus had just healed you of leprosy? What would you do?**

Say: **Although Jesus changed ten people's lives by healing their leprosy, only one took time to stop and thank him. This week when something good happens in your life, remember to stop and say thank you.**

Visual

Supplies: A large mixing bowl; water; white glue; hominy grits; a large paintbrush; a mirror (optional); and towels, washcloths, and soap (optional)

Preparation: Before class, mix equal parts of water, white glue, and hominy grits in a large mixing bowl.

Say: **To help us understand what leprosy looked like, I've prepared a mixture that will make our skin look like lepers' skin. The mixture won't hurt, and you can wash it off after class.**

Use a large paintbrush to paint the sticky mixture onto children's arms, hands, or faces. Be sure to ask children where they'd like you to apply their "leprosy."

After you've applied the mixture to everyone, talk with kids about how it feels to have leprosy. Invite them to describe the look and feel of their skin. If you've brought in a mirror, let kids look at themselves.

Let kids choose whether to wash off the mixture right away or to leave it on until the end of class. You may want to provide towels, washclothes, and soap for kids to wash off their leprosy. Say: **Fortunately, we can just wash our "leprosy" away. The lepers in Jesus' time had to live with their condition day in and day out. Good health is a blessing we can always be thankful for.**

VeRBal

Supplies: Paper and pencils

Preparation: none

Form groups of four, and give each group paper and pencils. Have each group write a story about one of the lepers. Have groups include these elements in their stories:
- the person's name and age,
- the person's background and family history,
- how the person got leprosy, and
- what the person did after being healed by Jesus.

If you choose to do the Physical activity, have groups use their stories to create dramas as described below. If you don't do the Physical activity, have groups read their stories to the class.

PHYSical

Supplies: Stories from the Verbal activity (optional)

Preparation: none

Form groups of four. (If you did the Verbal activity, use the same groups.) Have groups talk about the responses the lepers might have received when they returned home healed. Then have each group prepare a drama about a leper's homecoming. (If you did the Verbal activity, have kids incorporate details from their stories.)

Circulate among groups to offer help as needed. Encourage kids to consider different responses the lepers' families may have had, such as amazement, disbelief, relief, happiness, and excitement.

Allow no more than fifteen minutes for kids to prepare their dramas. Then have groups present their dramas to the rest of the class.

After all the dramas have been presented, say: **Jesus changed the lepers' lives in an amazing way. Jesus changes our lives in amazing ways, too. This week, tell a friend or family member about an amazing thing Jesus has done for you.**

MUSical

Supplies: none

Preparation: none

Give kids the beginning of this finger play. Have them complete the words to create a whole finger play about the ten lepers' story. Encourage kids to speak the words rhythmically—even in a rap style if they want.

After kids have finished the words for their finger play, help them add motions. Have kids practice the finger play until they know it well. Then have your class teach younger children the new finger play.

Logical

Supplies: Bibles, Bible reference materials such as Bible dictionaries and Bible encyclopedias, paper, pencils, newsprint, and markers

Preparation: Ask your pastor to help you gather Bible reference materials that will provide kids with information about leprosy. Your church may have books you can borrow. Local Christian schools might also be willing to loan out materials.

Set out Bibles and Bible reference materials, pencils, paper, newsprint, and markers. Have kids work in groups of three to develop presentations about what leprosy is, how people in the Bible treated lepers, and what the procedures were for dealing with lepers in Jesus' day.

Circulate among groups, and offer help as needed. Encourage kids to make their presentations as detailed as they want. For example, a group might draw a graph to show what percentage of people in Bible times had leprosy. Or a group might draw a picture of what leprous skin looked like. When kids complete their presentations, invite groups to volunteer to make their presentations for the rest of the class.

Reflective

Supplies: none

Preparation: none

Say: **Leprosy is very rare today—especially in developed countries. We don't have to worry about avoiding lepers. But sometimes we avoid people for other reasons. Every day we encounter people who aren't very nice, who look or smell different than we do, or who have different ideas. Sometimes it's hard to love people like that, just as it was hard for people in Bible times to love and accept lepers. Think of one person who is hard for you to get close to and love.**

Pause for one minute. Then say: **Jesus touched ten lepers with God's healing love. Think about how you can touch the difficult person you thought of with God's love.**

Pause for one minute and then close with a prayer similar to this one: "God, help us see beyond the outsides of people. Help us to touch people with your healing love. Amen."

● Play the song "Where Are the Other Nine?" by Geoff Moore. Have kids listen quietly to the music. Then have them work together to create a music video for the song. Videotape the music video, and show it to another class.

● Have kids dress in Bible-character costumes and paint each other's skin with the "leprosy" from the Visual activity. Take your costumed class to the mall, and have them perform one of the dramas they created in the Physical activity. (Be sure to obtain permission if necessary.) Have kids repeat the play every fifteen minutes for one to two hours. Take along information about your church for interested people.

EXTRA! EXTRA! EXTRA! EXTRA! EXTRA!

All Hope Is Gone

As they examine the events surrounding Jesus' death on the cross, kids will reflect on what Jesus' death means for them.

Musical

Supplies: A Bible; a hymnal or a recording of one of the following songs: "The Old Rugged Cross," "Lead Me to Calvary," "Beneath the Cross of Jesus," or "Crown Him With Many Crowns"; a CD or cassette player (if using a recording); a camcorder; a TV and a VCR; sample music videos (optional); popped popcorn; and bowls or bags

Preparation: Practice singing the song of your choice so you can teach it to kids. If you want to use recorded music, select a CD or cassette recording of the song you've chosen. (The cassette or CD *Hymns* by the Christian group Acapella has an upbeat version called "When I Survey/Old Rugged Cross" that kids might enjoy.) Set up a TV and a VCR. Make sure you know how to hook up the camcorder so you'll be able to play back the kids' video.

Have kids read Luke 23:1-56. Then have them create a music video for one of the songs listed above. Sing or play the song and then have kids work together to depict the song by acting it out or showing a story that illustrates the song. If you brought sample music videos, show them to the kids as idea-starters. Make sure all of the kids are involved in creating the video.

When kids are ready, videotape their music video. You might have some kids performing while others sing the song in the background. Then pop the video-tape in a VCR, bring out the popcorn, and let kids enjoy the Bible story through their own music video.

Visual

Supplies: Bibles, drawing paper, watercolor paints, paintbrushes, black crayons, toothpicks, old newspapers, and tape or pins

Preparation: Lay down old newspapers on the tables where kids will be working.

Set out drawing paper, watercolor paints, and paintbrushes. Have kids use the watercolor paints to cover their papers with color. While the paint is drying, have several volunteers take turns reading the Bible story from Luke 23:1-56.

Say: **When Jesus died, the sun stopped shining, and the whole land became dark for three hours. Use a black crayon to completely darken your papers.**

Set out black crayons, and let kids darken their papers. After kids have finished, read Luke 23:46. Say: **In the darkness, Jesus gave up his life. Use a toothpick to scratch out a picture of Jesus' death on the cross.**

Give kids toothpicks, and have them scratch out pictures of Jesus' death on the cross. Display the finished pictures on a wall or bulletin board.

 **VERBAL**

Supplies: Pencils and paper

Preparation: None. If you want, you could provide note cards and envelopes for kids to use in this activity.

Form groups of four. Give each group a sheet of paper and a pencil. Say: **When someone dies, people usually do kind things for that person's loved ones such as bringing food, sending flowers or cards expressing sympathy, or coming by to visit. After people do these kind things, the family sends thank-you cards.**

We're going to pretend that your group is Jesus' family. What would Jesus' family have said to the people who were kind or expressed sympathy when Jesus died? Imagine what people might have done back in those times as you write them thank-you notes. We're going to pretend that these were written the day after Jesus died, so Jesus' family doesn't know yet that Jesus will come back to life. For example, you might write: "Thank you for the green-olive and goat-cheese casserole you shared with our grieving family. We're still so upset that people killed our son and brother Jesus when he had done nothing wrong. Your kindness means so much. Sincerely, Jesus' family."

After kids have had time to write their thank-you notes, have groups take turns reading their notes to the rest of the class. Then say: **It must have been terrible for Jesus' family to see him suffer and die. Only Jesus knew that he would rise again after three days. It wasn't until after Jesus' resurrection that people understood that Jesus' death was part of God's plan for our sins to be forgiven. We can be thankful that we know the meaning of Jesus' death.**

LOGICAL

Supplies: Bibles and newsprint and a marker or a chalkboard and chalk

Preparation: Read the Scriptures kids will be studying in this activity. If you feel uncomfortable helping kids answer questions about Jesus' death, consider inviting your pastor or another church leader to join you for this activity.

Ask:
● **Why did Jesus have to die?**
Take several responses and then say: **To help us better understand why Jesus had to die, we're going to do an in-depth Bible study. We'll read Scripture passages together and discuss what each passage says about why Jesus had to die.**

Distribute Bibles, and read these passages: John 3:16-17; John 10:7-15; Romans 5:6-11; and Hebrews 9:11-15.

After you read each passage, ask:
● **What does this passage say about Jesus' death?**
● **What does this passage tell us about why Jesus died?**
● **What other questions does this passage create for you?**

Divide a sheet of newsprint or a chalkboard into three sections. Label the sections "What the Passage Says," "Why Jesus Died," and "Other Questions." As kids answer, have a scribe record each response on the appropriate section of the newsprint or chalkboard. After you've read all the passages, review the responses on the newsprint or chalkboard. Ask two or three children to tell in just a few sentences why Jesus had to die.

Encourage children to discuss with you or their parents any questions they have about Jesus' death and what it means.

PHYSICAL

Supplies: A Bible, a large block of wood, several 3-inch nails, and several hammers

Preparation: none

Have kids take turns hitting the nails into the block of wood with hammers. After everyone has had a turn, ask:
● **How does it feel to hammer a nail?**
● **How do you think it felt to the soldiers to hammer nails into Jesus' hands and feet?**
● **How do you think Jesus felt?**
Read aloud 1 Peter 2:21-24. Ask:
● **What does this passage mean?**
Say: **When Jesus was nailed to the cross, I think he looked down through the ages and saw each of your faces. He loved you so much that he wanted to die for you. It wasn't the nails that kept Jesus on the cross; it was his love for you.**

Jesus loves you and wants you to accept what he did for you on the cross. He wants to give you eternal life.

Some kids may want to talk more with you after class about how to accept Christ's forgiveness. If you're uncomfortable answering kids' questions, refer the questions to your pastor.

INTERPERSONAL

Supplies: Bibles

Preparation: Arrange for kids to display their freeze frame scenes as church members arrive for worship.

Form three groups, and give each group a Bible. Assign each group one of the following passages: Luke 23:13-25; Luke 23:33-49; and Luke 23:50-56. Have each group create a freeze frame scene that captures its part of the story. For example, kids may have one person hanging on a cross while others are frozen in motion around him.

Once kids complete their freeze frame scenes, move to an area where church members will see you as they arrive for worship. Have kids get into position. Tell kids not to move or talk until their presentation is over and everyone has passed by.

REFLECTIVE

Supplies: One nail for each child

Preparation: none

Give each child a nail to hold. Have kids close their eyes. Say: **As you hold**

this nail, think about Jesus' death and what he did for you. *(Pause.)* **Imagine Jesus seeing your face as he hung on the cross. What is he thinking?** *(Pause.)* **Spend time thinking about what Jesus endured for you.**

Allow three minutes of silence for kids to reflect. Let kids take their nails home with them as reminders of Jesus' death.

EXTRA! EXTRA! EXTRA! EXTRA! EXTRA!

● Play "Via Dolorosa" by Sandi Patti as background music during the Visual or Interpersonal activities.

● Have kids reenact Christ's death and burial and present their drama to another class.

● View *Shroud of Turin: Fraud or Evidence of Christ's Resurrection?* from the Ancient Secrets of the Bible video series (available from Group Publishing) as a class.

EXTRA! EXTRA! EXTRA! EXTRA! EXTRA!

A live Again!

Kids will

celebrate

Jesus' resurrec-

tion and dis-

cover how it

can change

their lives.

 MUSICAL

Supplies: A Bible; a piano, organ, or keyboard; and the sheet music for one of these hymns: "Christ Arose" or "Christ the Lord Is Risen Today."

Preparation: Arrange for someone to play one of the hymns listed in the Supplies section. (Choose which hymn you'll use.)

Take your children to an area of your church where a pianist or an organist can play the hymn you've selected. Read aloud Luke 24:1-49. Say: **Jesus' resurrection makes me want to celebrate! Let's celebrate together by singing a song about it.**

Lead kids in singing the hymn you've chosen. Then have kids work together to create choreography for the song. Arrange to have kids present their finished song in a future worship service.

 VERBAL

Supplies: Bibles

Preparation: none

Form three groups, and give each group a Bible. Have each group read 2 Corinthians 5:14-15 and discuss what it means. After five minutes, bring groups together and have them report on their discussions.

Then ask:

● **If you were living out these verses, how would you act in a fight with a friend?**

● **If you were living out these verses, how would you act when a parent tells you to do something you don't want to do?**

● **If you were living out these verses, how would you act when a friend who doesn't know Jesus is depressed?**

Let kids respond and then say: **Let's pray and ask Jesus to help us live out these verses this week. Lord Jesus, thank you for dying for us. Help us to live for you. Amen.**

VISUAL

Supplies: One plain T-shirt for each child, old newspapers, and fabric paints

Preparation: If you can't purchase T-shirts, announce this activity a week ahead and ask each child to bring a plain T-shirt to class the next week. You may want to call or send reminders to parents as well. Lay out old newspapers on the tables where kids will be working.

Set out the fabric paints, and give each child a plain T-shirt. Have kids use the fabric paints to create T-shirts that declare the Resurrection. Help kids create slogans such as "He arose!" "His pain, your gain," or "Jesus died for me. He is alive!" Have kids write their slogans on their T-shirts with the fabric paints.

Let the T-shirts dry before kids take them home. Encourage kids to wear their shirts to spread the good news about Jesus' resurrection.

LOGICAL

Supplies: Bibles

Preparation: none

Say: **Through the years since Christ's resurrection, many people have chosen not to believe that Jesus actually rose from the dead. And if you don't believe that Jesus rose from the dead, then Christianity is no different from any other religion. Some people believe that the Resurrection was a hoax—that someone stole Jesus' body. But Jesus appeared to his disciples several times after he rose from the dead.**

Turn to a partner and talk with him or her about the importance of the Resurrection in the Christian faith.

After five minutes, bring kids back together and have them report what they talked about. Say: **Together, Jesus' death and resurrection are critically important to our Christian faith. Jesus' death paid the price for our sins and allowed us to be forgiven. Jesus' resurrection shows that God has power over death and that God will someday raise Christians to live with him in heaven.**

Let's look at a Bible passage that helps confirm that Jesus really did rise from the dead.

Have kids sit with their partners. Give each pair a Bible, and have partners read 1 Corinthians 15:1-8 together. Ask the whole class:

● **How does it help us to know that all these people saw Jesus alive after the Crucifixion?**

Say: **After Jesus rose from the dead, his disciples risked their lives to spread the good news about Jesus' resurrection. Hundreds of people joined together to start the church. We can believe that Jesus is alive!**

PHYSICAL

Supplies: none

Preparation: none

Say: **Once you've experienced the new life Jesus' resurrection brings, you're never the same. We're going to celebrate the changed life Jesus gives us by playing a game called Resurrection Tag.**

Choose someone to be "It." Have It call out a motion such as hopping, skipping, or walking with giant steps. When It tags people, they are "changed," and they must do the new motion. Have It continue tagging people until everyone is changed.

Afterward, ask:

● **How has being touched by Jesus' resurrection changed you?**

● **Who can you touch with Jesus' love and resurrection power?**

Encourage kids to spread Jesus' love and resurrection power to the people they mention.

⊕ Reflective

Supplies: A Bible, newsprint and a marker or a chalkboard and chalk

Preparation: Write the words from Galatians 2:20 on the newsprint or chalkboard.

Point out the verse you've written on the newsprint or chalkboard. Tell kids to silently think about what this verse means for them. Give kids the following guidelines for their meditation.

Say: **As you reflect on the verse, think of what each word or phrase means. For example, "I" means me; God is talking about something for me to do. "Have been" is something that happened already. "Crucified" is another word for "killed."**

Every few words, stop and put the verse together in your own words. For example, you might say, "It's a fact that as a Christian, I have died."

Allow enough time for kids to really think about this verse.

Interpersonal

Supplies: Paper, pencils, and other craft supplies (optional)

Preparation: none

Form pairs, and give kids paper and pencils. Set out the other craft supplies if you're providing them.

Say: **Jesus' resurrection is good news! We need to always remember that God sent his only Son to die for us.**

Have pairs brainstorm good-news symbols, such as an empty cross or a bright, shining star. Then have each child create or draw a good-news symbol to present to his or her partner. Tell kids to take their symbols home and keep them as a reminder of the good news of Christ's death and resurrection.

Extra! Extra! Extra! Extra! Extra!

● Rent and watch the movie *Jesus*.

● To discover more evidence about Jesus' death and resurrection, help kids study selections from Josh McDowell's book, *Evidence That Demands a Verdict*.

● Make snacks from layered gelatin squares that tell the Gospel story. Layer red for Jesus' death, yellow (gold) for eternal life, and green for growth as a Christian. Tell the story to children when you serve this treat.

Extra! Extra! Extra! Extra! Extra!

# **H**old Everything!

As they examine
Lazarus'
resurrection,
kids will discover
how Jesus'
miracles
brought glory to
God.

Verbal

Supplies: A Bible, pencils, and paper

Preparation: none

Read aloud John 11:1-44. Say: **When someone dies, the local newspaper prints an obituary for the person. An obituary is a short article about the person who died.**

Let's imagine that there was a newspaper in Lazarus' town called The Bethany Chronicle. Lazarus and his family are now facing a dilemma. Lazarus died and the paper announced the death, but now Lazarus is alive. Jesus raised him from the dead. How can Lazarus and his family let people know about the miracle?

Form pairs, and give pairs pencils and paper. Have partners work together to write letters to the editor explaining what has happened to Lazarus. Afterward, have several volunteers read their letters for the class.

Ask:
● **What do you think people thought when Lazarus came back to life?**
● **What would you have thought?**

Say: **It's amazing to think that one day Lazarus was dead and buried and the next day he was up walking around. Raising Lazarus was one of Jesus' greatest miracles. And like all his miracles, it was performed to give glory to God.**

Visual

Supplies: An old sheet, scissors, and a bowl of dirt

Preparation: none

Choose one person to be Lazarus. Set out an old sheet, scissors, and a bowl of dirt. Have kids work together to demonstrate what Lazarus may have looked like when he came out of the tomb. For example, kids might wrap up Lazarus with strips of the sheet and then rub dirt on the strips. Encourage kids to collaborate with Lazarus as they work. Make sure they don't do anything that will make Lazarus uncomfortable.

When kids finish wrapping Lazarus, read Jesus' words from John 11:44b:
" **'Take the cloth off of him and let him go.' "**

Have kids celebrate the resurrection of Lazarus by tearing the sheet off of him or her.

MUSICAL

Supplies: none

Preparation: none

Ask children to describe funerals they've been to. If no one has been to a funeral, describe one that you've been to. Then ask: **What is the music at a funeral like?**

Say: **If Lazarus died today, what kind of music would be played at his funeral? Let's choose three songs that we'd want to have played at his funeral.**

When a child suggests a song, have him or her sing a few lines so others will recognize it. After all the suggestions, choose three funeral songs for Lazarus' funeral. Then have kids choose one celebration-type song for Lazarus' return to life. Sing all the songs together as a celebration of Jesus' miracle.

LOGICAL

Supplies: none

Preparation: Arrange for a mortician or funeral director to visit your class. If you can't get a mortician to visit your class, tape-record or videotape an interview with a mortician.

Introduce your guest, and invite him or her to talk to kids about what a mortician does today. Then ask your guest to comment on the embalming and burial process in Jesus' day. Encourage kids to ask questions if they want to. Remind your guest to be sensitive to impressionable younger children.

After the live or taped presentation, ask:

● **How did Jesus raise Lazarus from the dead?**

● **Why did Jesus raise Lazarus from the dead?**

● **Does Lazarus' resurrection in any way make Jesus' resurrection not seem so great? Why or why not?**

Say: **Jesus raised Lazarus from the dead to demonstrate God's power—to prove to people that he was indeed God's Son. Even after this great miracle, some people didn't believe Jesus and began making plans to have him arrested and killed. They didn't understand that Jesus' death was part of God's plan. Jesus' death and resurrection proved that he was God's Son.**

PHYSICAL

Supplies: Three rolls of bathroom tissue

Preparation: none

Form three teams. Have each team choose one person to be Lazarus. Give each team a roll of bathroom tissue. When you say "Go," have each team use its roll of tissue to race the others in wrapping up its Lazarus. Then tell the Lazaruses to "come forth" by bursting out of their bathroom-tissue wraps.

INTERPERSONAL

Supplies: A Bible, a roll of bathroom tissue, and pens

Preparation: none

Read aloud Ephesians 2:1-5. Say: **We may be physically alive, but all of us are spiritually dead if we don't have Jesus as our Savior. When Jesus died on the cross, he gave us new life in him if we accept his gift.**

If we have the new life Jesus gives us, we live our lives differently. Instead of doing the things the world wants us to do, we do the things Jesus wants us to do.

Ask:

● **What are some things Jesus wants us to do?**

Distribute pens and bathroom-tissue squares, and say: **Using a pen and bathroom-tissue squares, write ways that you see this Jesus-kind of new life in people in our group. For example, you may write, "Tiffany, you never get mad" or "Blake, you praise God always." Make as many squares as you like and then deliver them to the people you wrote about.**

Have kids make and deliver their new-life squares. Then thank God for the new life we have in Jesus.

REFLECTIVE

Supplies: A Bible, bathroom tissue, and pens

Preparation: none

Read aloud Psalm 27:14. Say: **Lazarus and his sisters had to wait for Jesus to work a wonderful miracle for them. What does it mean to "wait for the Lord's help"?**

Have kids think silently about areas in which they need to trust and wait for God to help them. Distribute pens and bathroom-tissue squares, and have kids write the areas they thought of on bathroom-tissue squares. Have kids take the squares home as a reminder to trust God.

EXTRA! EXTRA! EXTRA! EXTRA! EXTRA!

● Play Carmen's song "Lazarus, Come Forth." Have kids close their eyes while the music plays and imagine what it would have been like to see Lazarus come out of the tomb.

● Have kids think of an ongoing ministry they can do for people in your church who are grieving. Kids may decide to send handmade cards, deliver baked goods, or call to offer their prayers and support. Help kids with their ministry whenever necessary.

EXTRA! EXTRA! EXTRA! EXTRA! EXTRA!

I Saw the Light

As they hear how Paul's life was changed by an encounter with Jesus, kids will discover that Jesus can change their lives, too.

LoGiCal

Supplies: Bibles, pencils, and paper

Preparation: Read the Scriptures kids will study in this activity.

Read aloud Acts 9:1-22. Say: **This story tells us how Saul changed from an enemy to a follower of Jesus. After Saul's change of heart, he was called Paul. Let's find out more about his change of heart by reading about Saul and Paul.**

Form two groups, and give each group Bibles, pencils, and paper. Have one group read Acts 7:51–8:3 and the other group read Philippians 3:5-14. Based on what they read, have the Acts group list the "old Saul" characteristics and the Philippians group list the "new Paul" characteristics.

Then bring groups together, and have them compare their lists. Afterward, ask:

● **What were the biggest changes Jesus made in Paul?**
● **Why did Paul change so radically?**
● **What's one way Jesus has changed you?**

Close with a prayer similar to this one: "Lord Jesus, thank you for loving us. Your love changes our lives. Help us to live out your love this week. Amen."

PHYSiCal

Supplies: A Bible and a flashlight

Preparation: Clear away any obstacles that kids could trip over when you darken the room.

Say: **Paul became a Christian because Jesus sought him out. It took a blinding light and a personal appearance from the risen Jesus to get Paul's attention. Let's play a game of Light and Seek to help us remember Paul's story.**

Choose one person to be "It." Have It cover his or her eyes while the other children find hiding places in your room. When everyone is hidden, darken the room and give It a flashlight. When It shines his or her light on someone, that person must come out and help It look for the others. Play the game several times.

Then ask:

● **What was it like when It shone the light on you?**
● **How was the light like or unlike the light that blinded Paul?**

Read John 8:12. Say: **Paul was blinded by a physical light, but we can show the light of Jesus' love in other ways.**

Ask:

● **How can you show Jesus' light to someone this week?**

Encourage kids to do the things they suggested.

VISUAL

Supplies: Food coloring, glue, bowls, craft sticks, and wax paper

Preparation: Just before class, mix a few drops of food coloring into several tablespoons of glue. Make at least four different colors. Put a different color of glue in each bowl.

Ask:
- **Who can tell me the life cycle of a caterpillar?**

Say: **When the caterpillar hatches out of its cocoon, it's no longer a caterpillar. The plain caterpillar becomes a completely different creature—a beautiful butterfly. Just as the caterpillar's life changes, our lives change when we put our faith in Jesus. Listen to what the Bible says about that.**

Read aloud 2 Corinthians 5:17. Ask:
- **What does this verse mean?**
- **According to this verse, how are we like caterpillars?**

Say: **When we decide to follow Jesus, we become changed people. Today we're learning how the Apostle Paul was dramatically changed when he put his faith in Christ. Let's make "new creation" butterflies to help us remember that we're new creations in Christ.**

Set out the craft sticks and bowls of colored glue. Give each child a sheet of wax paper. Have kids create butterflies by spreading the colored glue on their wax paper in butterfly shapes using craft sticks. Help each child to make sure each color he or she uses is touching the other colors on his or her butterfly.

Once the glue dries, kids can peel their butterflies off the wax paper. The smooth side of each butterfly will stick to a window. Encourage kids to put the butterflies on their bedroom windows to remind them of their new life in Christ.

MUSICAL

Supplies: Strobe lights or a flashlight, written lyrics or a CD or cassette recording of "Amazing Grace," and a CD or cassette player (if using recording)

Preparation: Cover the windows in your room if necessary to make it as dark as possible.

Say: **The light was turned on for Paul when he met Jesus on the road to Damascus. We're going to create a light show to go along with the song "Amazing Grace."**

Choose several kids to act out Paul's encounter with Jesus. You'll need a Paul, a Jesus, an Ananias, and several spectators. While the actors are preparing their parts, lead the rest of the class in singing "Amazing Grace."

Once everyone has their parts down, have your "choir" stand at one side of the room. Have your actors stand in the center of the room. Turn off the lights, and turn on your strobe lights or flash your flashlight. Have your choir sing "Amazing Grace" as the actors act out the story in slow motion.

Your kids may want to present their show to parents or another class.

Reflective

Supplies: Bibles, pencils, and paper

Preparation: none

Give each child a Bible, paper, and a pencil. Say: **Paul actively shared his faith after he believed in Christ. He wanted to tell everyone what Christ had done for him.**

Have volunteers read aloud Acts 22:1-22. Say: **These verses tell Paul's story. Take a few minutes to write your own story about how Christ has changed you. Include a "before I met Christ" section, a "placing my faith in Christ" section, and a "how he has changed me" section.**

Allow at least ten minutes for kids to write their stories. Encourage kids to keep their stories in their Bibles as reminders of their faith.

Interpersonal

Supplies: Faith stories from the Reflective activity or newsprint and a marker

Preparation: If you didn't do the Reflective activity, write the following questions on newsprint or a chalkboard, and post them where kids can see them.
● Where were you when you first heard about Jesus?
● Who was the first person to talk to you about Jesus?
● When did you decide to put your faith in Jesus?
● What actions did you take as a result of your decision?
● How is your life different now as a result of knowing Jesus?

Form pairs. Have partners share the faith stories they wrote in the Reflective activity with each other, or have partners ask each other the questions printed on the newsprint or chalkboard.

After pairs have discussed the questions or their faith stories, invite partners to share their responses with the class. For fun, have each partner describe the other partner's faith.

Verbal

Supplies: Pencils, paper, and Bible-character costumes and props (optional)

Preparation: none

Form groups of three, and give each group pencils and paper. Say: **When Paul was in Damascus after seeing the Lord's vision, he met a man named Ananias. Ananias was sent by God to help Paul to see the Holy Spirit. We can be like Ananias by helping people we know who are struggling with their faith to understand what it means to follow God. In your groups, brainstorm a situation in which you could be an "Ananias." For example, you may think of standing with a friend who is tempted to bow to peer pressure or of telling a friend who is struggling with a tough time about God's love for them.**

Give groups about five minutes to brainstorm their situations and then have them put together role-plays to present their situations to the class. Provide Bible-character costumes and props if you have them.

After kids have presented their role-plays to the class, have kids give each other a big round of applause.

EXTRA! EXTRA! EXTRA! EXTRA! EXTRA!

● Have kids create a life-size mural that tells the story of Paul meeting Jesus on the road to Damascus. Create your mural on a classroom wall or a long sheet of newsprint.

● Have kids interview people in your church to discover their faith stories and how they met Christ.

EXTRA! EXTRA! EXTRA! EXTRA! EXTRA!

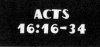

Jailhouse Rock

Kids will be challenged to stand up for their faith as they hear about Paul and Silas' prison experience.

Visual

Supplies: A Bible, newsprint, markers, empty cardboard tubes from wrapping paper or paper towels, paper bags, tape, and old newspapers

Preparation: none

Read aloud Acts 16:16-34. Ask:
● **What do you think the jail that Paul and Silas were in looked like? smelled like? sounded like?**
Say: **You're going to create a jail cell in this corner of our room. Use the supplies I've set out to create your jail cell.**
Set out the supplies you've brought. Encourage kids to involve everyone as they work. If kids get stumped, suggest that they add stone walls (paper bags stuffed with newspaper and taped shut), rats (tape wads colored gray), prison-cell bars (cardboard tubes and tape), a window, and graffiti.
After kids complete their jail cell, have everyone sit in it as you discuss the following questions:
● **How would you have felt to be locked up for being a Christian?**
● **What would you do if you were imprisoned for your faith?**
● **What does Paul and Silas' reaction tell us about them?**
Say: **We may never be locked up as Paul and Silas were, but we can still learn from their example. If you have trouble standing up for your faith, remember Paul and Silas. God took care of them—he'll take care of you, too.**

Verbal

Supplies: A Bible

Preparation: none

Form pairs. Read aloud Acts 16:25-34. Say: **After the jailer put his faith in Christ, he took Paul and Silas home with him and his entire family also believed. Talk with your partner about what you think the jailer may have said to his family.**
After three minutes, ask kids to act out what they talked about. Have partners choose who'll be the jailer and who'll be the jailer's wife or child. Have pairs take turns presenting their "Jailer's Homecoming" skits.

Physical

Supplies: A large key (optional)

Preparation: Clear your room of furniture and other obstacles. If possible, plan to play this game outside or in a gymnasium or fellowship hall.

Say: **After the earthquake, the jailer was a busy man. He had to survey the damage to the jail, pick up broken chains and other debris, and check to see that no prisoners had escaped—all in the middle of the night. Let's play a game that will help us imagine how confused the jailer may have been.**

Choose one person to be the jailer. Have the rest of the kids form two teams. On each team, have half of the kids be Pauls and the other half be Silases. Have teams stand on opposite ends of the room. Have the jailer stand in the center of the room. If you've brought a key, give it to the jailer.

Each time you call out "Paul" or "Silas," the Pauls or Silases on each team must switch places. If a child is tagged by the jailer as he or she crosses the room, the tagged child must go and sit in a designated "jail area" (on the sidelines or in a corner of the room). If you call out "Earthquake!" everyone must switch places, and kids who are in the jail area may also attempt to return to their teams. For added fun, play music during this game.

Play for about ten minutes. Choose a new jailer every two minutes. End the game by calling out "All here!" and having kids sit down where they are. Have the current jailer count heads to make sure everyone's accounted for before continuing with your lesson.

🎵 Musical

Supplies: none

Preparation: Arrange for your church's worship leader to lead your class in several praise songs. Offer to provide any supplies he or she may request, such as an overhead projector and a screen or a CD or cassette player.

Say: **Paul and Silas were in trouble. They'd been arrested, beaten, and thrown in jail. But rather than complain or get depressed, they focused on God. When we focus on God and praise him, God will do great things to lift us out of our problems.**

Have your worship leader lead the children in singing several praise songs. Close your worship time by thanking God for helping kids with their problems.

±⁼ Logical

Supplies: Paper and pencils

Preparation: If possible, arrange for kids to complete their miracle reports by visiting adult classes that meet at the same time as yours.

Ask:
● **How big of a miracle was it for God to send an earthquake to free Paul and Silas from prison?**
● **What things about an event are necessary in order for it to be considered a miracle?**
● **Have you ever had a miracle happen to you? Explain.**

For this activity, you can either send kids out to adult classes or have them complete the project during the week. Either way, have kids interview people until each child finds someone who has experienced a miracle. When kids find people who have experienced miracles, have them ask those people the following questions:

- What was your miracle?
- Why do you think it's a miracle?
- What would you say to someone who says that your miracle could have happened without God's help?

Have kids write down people's responses and then return to your class with their miracle reports. Have kids give their reports one at a time. Afterward, discuss how their research has helped shape what they think constitutes a miracle.

 # Interpersonal

Supplies: Paper, pens, and tape

Preparation: Write each child's name on a separate sheet of paper. Tape the papers on the wall at kids' eye-level.

Say: **People knew that Paul and Silas were Christians. Their lives had lots of evidence that could convict them of loving and believing in Jesus. Your lives show lots of evidence of loving and believing in Jesus too.**

In just a minute, we're going to list some of that evidence. We'll walk around the room and write on each person's paper evidences we've seen of that person's faith in Christ. For example, you may write, "prays about problems," "comes to church," or "is kind to people." Let's fill up each other's papers with evidence.

Give each child a pen. Join kids as they walk around and write encouraging evidences of faith on each other's papers. Make sure each child writes something on each paper. When everyone has finished writing, have children remove and read their papers.

 # Reflective

Supplies: A Bible

Preparation: none

Say: **Paul and Silas were willing to give up their freedom for their faith in Christ. I'm going to read some things that you may be asked to give up for your faith in Christ. Don't say anything, but silently answer yes or no to each question.**

Would you still believe in Jesus if...
- **your best friend said to choose Jesus or your friendship with him or her.**
- **kids at school laughed at you.**
- **your teacher gave you a bad grade for saying you believed in Jesus.**
- **people threw rocks at your house because you're a Christian.**
- **your family was jailed for being Christians.**
- **someone threatened to kill you if you wouldn't reject Christ.**

Read aloud Matthew 5:10-12. Then pray that God will give kids courage to stand up for their faith, even when it's hard.

EXTRA! EXTRA! EXTRA! EXTRA! EXTRA!

- Play Elvis Presley's "Jailhouse Rock." Have kids work to put the Bible story to this tune.

- View the "Earthquake" song section of the *Donut Hole Two* video (available from Gospel Light).

EXTRA! EXTRA! EXTRA! EXTRA! EXTRA!

Shipwrecked

As they hear how Paul was shipwrecked, kids will learn that God watches over those who trust him, even in trying times.

Musical

Supplies: Bibles and props for making sound effects, such as hymnals, fans, rhythm instruments, paper, or other items that are readily available in your church or classroom

Preparation: none

Distribute Bibles, and say: **We're going to create sound effects for today's Bible story. Read Acts 27:27-44, and work together to create sound effects for the story.**

Have kids form groups, and allow groups to find sound-making props around your church as long as they return them when they're finished. Encourage kids to read Acts 27:27-44 to determine what sound effects they'll create for the story.

Once kids have created their sound effects, read aloud Acts 27:27–44. Pause as needed for kids to make their sound effects during the story.

Visual

Supplies: One two-liter soft drink bottle with a lid for each child, aluminum foil, water, blue food coloring, cooking oil, and a measuring cup

Preparation: none

Say: **Paul experienced a frightening shipwreck. Let's make not-so-frightening miniature shipwrecks to help us remember how God helped him.**

Have kids peel the labels off their bottles. Then have each child shape a ship, sea creatures, and people out of aluminum foil that will fit through the opening in his or her bottle. Help kids put their aluminum foil sculptures into their bottles. Fill each bottle two-thirds full of water. Add blue food coloring and one-half cup cooking oil to each bottle. Have kids put the lids on their bottles and shake their miniature seas to create their own shipwrecks.

Verbal

Supplies: Paper and pencils

Preparation: none

Form groups of four. Have each child imagine he or she was the first mate on the ship when it wrecked. Have them pretend they were standing next to Paul the entire time. Have groups write accounts of the shipwreck from the first mate's perspective. When groups finish their stories, have kids take turns reading them to each other.

Then say: **God intervened in Paul's life in an amazing way. Because of Paul's faith, the ship's officers and all the passengers were saved from drowning.**

Ask:

● **When has God intervened to save you or someone you know from danger?**

● **How has your faith in God "kept you afloat" when tough things happened?**

Close by having groups pray together. Encourage kids to thank God for watching over them, and ask God to strengthen their faith.

L⊙Gical

Supplies: Bibles and two Bible concordances or topical Bibles

Preparation: If possible, arrange for your pastor to join you for this activity.

Read aloud Acts 28:1-5, and say: **Paul could have died when his ship broke up after fourteen days of stormy weather. But Paul wasn't injured in the shipwreck. Instead, he swam safely to shore. After he reached land, a snake crawled out of the fire and latched onto Paul's arm. But Paul wasn't injured by the snake, either. God protected Paul because of his faith. Listen to what the Bible says about God's protection.**

Read aloud Psalm 34:15-20. Say: **We're going to debate this passage. This half of the room** (to your left) **will argue that this passage is saying that if we have faith, we'll never be harmed. The other half of the room** (to your right) **will argue that that's not what the Bible is saying. Provide Bible verses to support your argument.**

Give each group several Bibles and a concordance or topical Bible. Allow groups fifteen to twenty minutes to prepare. Circulate between groups as needed to help kids find verses to support their arguments. Then hold your debate.

You may want to have your pastor attend the debate and give a closing summary of this issue.

Physical

Supplies: none

Preparation: Clear your room of furniture and other obstacles. If possible, arrange to play this game outside or in a gymnasium or fellowship hall.

Lead kids in a game of Shipwreck Tag. Choose someone to be the "storm." Then form groups of three. Call each group a "ship." Have kids in each ship form a line by having each child place his or her hands on the hips of the person in front of him or her. During the game, kids forming each ship must stay connected and run from the storm. If the storm touches a ship, that ship is shipwrecked. Then kids in the shipwrecked ship must let go of each other and form new ships of three with kids from other shipwrecked ships. Have shipwrecked kids stand on the sideline until they can form new ships with other kids.

Play the game for five minutes. Choose a new storm every minute. After the game, say: **When the storm touched your ship, you broke apart and became shipwrecked. Troubles and stormy times can "shipwreck" us in real life, too. But if we have faith, God will guide us through the storms.**

Interpersonal

Supplies: none

Preparation: none

Form a large circle. Tell about the hardest or scariest thing you've ever faced and how God was there for you. Then go around the circle, and have each child tell about a personal difficult experience and how God was there for him or her through the experience. After everyone has shared, close with a prayer of thanks to God.

Reflective

Supplies: none

Preparation: none

Say: **Think of someone you know who is on the verge of a shipwreck. Maybe this person is tempted to give in to peer pressure and do something wrong. Or maybe someone you know is about to get a divorce. We're going to spend time in silent prayer, asking God to help those people.**

Allow kids to pray silently for three minutes, then close with a brief prayer of thanks for God's faithful answers to prayer.

EXTRA! EXTRA! EXTRA! EXTRA! EXTRA!

● Say: **An angel spoke to Paul and told him that God would save the 276 people on the ship.** Ask: **Do you think God still speaks to people through angels? Why or why not? What is an angel's job?**

Read aloud Hebrews 13:2. Ask: **Have you ever thought that you met an angel? Explain.**

Say: **Angels are God's ministering spirits. Angels serve God and worship him.**

Read aloud Psalm 34:7. Ask: **What does the angel of the Lord do for us?**

Say: **The Bible only gives us a little bit of information about angels. We don't know exactly what they looked like or if we'll ever see one here on earth. But we know they watched over Paul and that they watch over us today.**

● Have each child pretend that he or she was the centurion on the ship. Have kids work together to write a report to the centurion's commander about the shipwreck.

EXTRA! EXTRA! EXTRA! EXTRA! EXTRA!

Evaluation of FORGET-ME-NOT BIBLE STORY ACTIVITIES

Please help Group Publishing continue to provide innovative and usable resources for ministry by taking a moment to fill out and send us this evaluation. Thanks!

● ● ●

1. As a whole, this book has been (circle one):

Not much help   Very helpful

1   2   3   4   5   6   7   8   9   10

2. The things I liked best about this book were:

3. This book could be improved by:

4. One thing I'll do differently because of this book is:

5. Optional Information:

Name _____

Street Address _____

City _____ State _____ Zip _____

Phone Number _____ Date _____

BRING THE BIBLE TO LIFE FOR YOUR 1st- THROUGH 6th-GRADERS WITH GROUP'S HANDS-ON BIBLE CURRICULUM™

Energize your kids with Active Learning!

Group's **Hands-On Bible Curriculum**™ will help you teach the Bible in a radical new way. It's based on Active Learning—the same teaching method Jesus used.

In each lesson, students will participate in exciting and memorable learning experiences using fascinating gadgets and gizmos you've not seen with any other curriculum. Your elementary students will discover biblical truths and <u>remember</u> what they learn—because they're <u>doing</u> instead of just listening.

You'll save time and money too!

While students are learning more, you'll be working less—simply follow the quick and easy instructions in the **Teachers Guide**. You'll get tons of material for an energy-packed 35- to 60-minute lesson. And, if you have extra time, there's an arsenal of Bonus Ideas and Time Stuffers to keep kids occupied—and learning! Plus, you'll SAVE BIG over other curriculum programs that require you to buy expensive separate student books—all student handouts in Group's **Hands-On Bible Curriculum** are photocopiable!

In addition to the easy-to-use **Teachers Guide**, you'll get all the essential teaching materials you need in a ready-to-use **Learning Lab®**. No more running from store to store hunting for lesson materials—all the active-learning tools you need to teach 13 exciting Bible lessons to any size class are provided for you in the **Learning Lab**.

Challenging topics each quarter keep your kids coming back!

Group's **Hands-On Bible Curriculum** covers topics that matter to your kids and teaches them the Bible with integrity. Switching topics every month keeps your 1st- through 6th-graders enthused and coming back for more. The full two-year program will help your kids...

> ❧ make God-pleasing decisions,
> ❧ recognize their God-given potential, and
> ❧ seek to grow as Christians.

Take the boredom out of Sunday school, children's church, and youth group for your elementary students. Make your job easier and more rewarding with no-fail lessons that are ready in a flash. Order Group's **Hands-On Bible Curriculum** for your 1st- through 6th-graders today.

Hands-On Bible Curriculum is also available for Toddlers & 2s, Preschool, and Pre-K and K!

PRACTICAL RESOURCES FOR YOUR CHILDREN'S MINISTRY

The Children's Worker's Encyclopedia of Bible-Teaching Ideas
New ways to present the Bible—at your fingertips!

Captivate even children who have grown up in church with over 340 attention-grabbing, active-learning devotions. . . art and craft projects. . . creative prayers. . . service projects. . . field trips. . . music suggestions. . . quiet reflection activities. . . skits. . . and more. You'll find winning ideas from every book of the Bible! Directions are simple and crystal clear, so it's easy to slide an idea in any time—on short notice—with little or no preparation. And handy indexes outlining ideas by Scripture, theme, and idea style make it easy to find exactly the right idea on a moment's notice!

Old Testament   ISBN 1-55945-622-1
New Testament   ISBN 1-55945-625-6

Quick Children's Sermons: Will My Dog Be in Heaven?

Kids ask the most *amazing* questions—and now you'll be ready to answer 50 of them! You'll get witty, wise, and biblically solid answers to kid-sized questions. . . and each question and answer makes a *wonderful* children's sermon. You'll know what to say when you hear questions like: "What color shoes does God like?" "Will God still love me if I don't eat my broccoli?" and more. Here's an attention-grabbing resource for children's pastors, Sunday school teachers, church workers, and parents.

ISBN 1-55945-612-4

Incredible Edible Bible Fun
Nanette Goings

Roll up your sleeves for more than 50 kid-friendly, teacher-approved recipes that make learning fun *and* tasty! Each recipe ties to a simple, age-appropriate devotion or project. And children will stir up their creations safely and quickly—you won't need any sharp knives, hot ovens, or refrigerators. And each recipe takes just 20 minutes from start to finish.

ISBN 0-7644-2001-1

"Show Me!" Devotions for Leaders to Teach Kids
Susan L. Lingo

Here are all the eye-catching science tricks, sleight-of-hand stunts, and illusions that kids love learning so they can flabbergast adults. . . but now there's an even *better* reason to know them! Each amazing trick is an illustration for an "Oh, Wow!" devotion that drives home a memorable Bible truth. And here's a twist: You'll train your children to share these devotions with others! **"Show Me!" Devotions** are simple enough for an all-thumbs 1st-grader (or teacher!), but slick enough to prompt a playground of 5th-graders to stop for the show—and then hear about Jesus.

ISBN 0-7644-2022-4

MORE PRACTICAL RESOURCES FOR YOUR CHILDREN'S MINISTRY

Bible Story Crafts & Projects Children Love

Discover creative art and craft ideas that reinforce 10 Old and 10 New Testament Bible stories...and help you bring the Bible to life for elementary children! And these are **fun** crafts! *Edible* crafts...*wearable* crafts...sculpting and modeling crafts...and even cooperative projects that will stay in—and decorate—your classroom! The very best ideas from outstanding teachers across the country—using easily gathered materials—now in one place! So roll up your sleeves—and tell your kids to get ready for fun as you teach them truths from God's Word in ways they'll really remember!

ISBN 1-55945-698-1

Instant Games for Children's Ministry
Susan L. Lingo

Play 101 use-'em-anywhere games—and it's as easy as 1...2...3!

1. Collect 14 inexpensive, everyday items such as two Ping-Pong balls... a bag of balloons...two bandannas...things that are a snap to find!
2. Drop the items in bag, and...
3. You're ready!

You'll always be prepared with a fun activity...action-packed game...or child-pleasing party idea! They're in the bag—ready at a moment's notice! Games come complete with instructions...rules...and quick and easy explanations so you'll have your children laughing and playing in no time!

ISBN 1-55945-695-7

No-Work Paperwork for Children's Ministry

Take the headache out of planning...prep time...and administration with over 100 easy-to-use, quick-copy forms you'll *never* need to write again for...

- Recruiting volunteers...
- Tracking expenses...
- Getting parents' permissions...
- Organizing events...and
- Staying on top of calendars, checklists, requests, and reminders.

Use these fast forms to stay organized...keep tabs on your budget...and cover legal requirements that come with children's ministry. Plus, you'll have more time to work with kids!

ISBN 1-55945-621-3